BEYOND THE CLOUDS

Beyond the Clouds

Coping with Pain and Disillusionment

Laurence Singlehurst

With contributions by Justyn Singlehurst

Hodder & Stoughton
LONDON SYDNEY AUCKLAND

Copyright © 2002 by Laurence Singlehurst

First published in Great Britain 2002

The right of Laurence Singlehurst to be identified as the Author of the Work has been asserted by him in accordance with the Copyright, Designs and Patents Act 1988.

10 9 8 7 6 5 4 3 2 1

British Library Cataloguing in Publication Data
A record for this book is available from the British Library

ISBN 0 340 78528 4

Typeset by Avon Dataset Ltd, Bidford-on-Avon, Warks

Printed and bound in Great Britain by
Clays Ltd, St Ives plc

Hodder and Stoughton Ltd
A Division of Hodder Headline Ltd
338 Euston Road
London NW1 3BH

Contents

Foreword

As a doctor trained in the care of the dying I have often seen people at times of immense personal suffering and sadness, with pain in family relationships. At such times it is normal to ask questions and to be angry, sad, frustrated, anxious. It's also normal to be accepting, at peace and with an intense sense of the presence of God, or to find all these emotions mixed up together. Other kinds of personal crisis can trigger a similar process. We struggle to find answers and can find our faith tested to the uttermost.

This book starts with a brutally honest account of family traumas in the home of a high-profile Christian leader, detailing what happened, how it affected each of them in different ways and how they came through a trial of fire to find a new sense of mission and purpose.

Laurence Singlehurst's account shook me when I first read it, and his son's own closing remarks moved me to tears. This book tells life as it really is; it takes us to the depths and brings us up again with a new sense of hope in our hearts.

However, the issue is about far more than just family relationships; it's about how those who have faith in Christ handle suffering of all kinds. It's about finding God in the pain, when prayers seem unheard and God's favour seems withdrawn. It's about the cry of the heart, from the very depths of our being, when troubles overwhelm us. It's about reconnecting with the One who made all, and is in all, and knows all.

As Christians we can be swift to judge when things seem to go wrong. We judge others, perhaps believing deep down (despite what we say) that people living God's way are especially protected from the trials of life. In my experience, Christians are often quick also to judge themselves. This is particularly true when it comes to family life. Parents tend to feel responsible for everything that happens, and this can swiftly become an intense burden of guilt.

The gospel message seems to have become: 'Give your life to Jesus Christ, and you will be protected from illness, early death, redundancy, or any other of the normal perils of day to day existence.' For example, the usual reaction in many churches to the diagnosis of cancer of a child is: 'How could God allow this?'

But my own reading of the Scriptures leads me to a very different place. In the first words of Paul's second letter to the Corinthians he tells us that God comforts us in all our troubles, so that we in turn can share with others the consolation we have received from Christ. 'If distress be our lot, it is the price we pay for your consolation, for your salvation' (2 Corinthians 1:6, New English Bible).

If coming to Christ means permanent immunity from painful experiences, then what earthly use will we possibly be to those who are still to find faith for themselves? We will have nothing to say. Paul also tells us in his letter to the Romans that 'suffering trains us to endure, and endurance brings proof that we have stood the test, and this proof is the ground of hope' (Romans 5:3–4, New English Bible).

If the reason you and I are still on earth is to influence others, to spread the Good News, to help bring about the coming of His Kingdom, then anything that assists this is good and that which hinders is bad. We see that our own suffering connects us to others in their point of need, at a time when they themselves may be most open to God's love and purpose. Because we have been through difficult times, we have something to say to those whose trial is now. We bring hope, a ray of light.

And another thing: we know that the times we pray most, when we are most in need of the sense of God's presence, are periods when we feel vulnerable, under huge pressures and empty of our own strength. So our own suffering not only opens doors to the hearts of others but also keeps us spiritually strong. This is a profound truth. Suffering is essential for our own good. And we see the fruit in all those who have suffered much. There is a strength of spirit, a nobleness of character – unless suffering has twisted the spirit into cynicism and hardness. How could we imagine someone like Nelson Mandela arising in a future generation, without a life-time walk of suffering and personal pain?

There will always be questions about how a God of love can allow suffering, but it is not an issue that has ever troubled me, even though perhaps I have seen at first hand more human suffering than most, both in illness and in global poverty.

Laurence deals with this complex issue in some depth, so I make just brief observations.

First, the pain of loss is a great source of suffering, but you cannot have love without grief. The pain of parting is a direct result of the joy of being together. The greater the joy, the greater the suffering. So what would you rather: a world without love or a world without grief? We choose every day the way of love, to allow other people to become important to us, and in doing so make ourselves vulnerable to future pain.

Second, life on earth only has meaning if it is a journey with choices. Otherwise you and I are mere automatons. For the whole of eternity we will be actively worshipping God, so worship, praise and adoration are weak reasons for our daily existence here. You and I are breathing air today because in God's great wisdom and purpose He has entrusted us with a mission, a task that can only be completed here on earth. That mission is to influence and to seek to change the choices made by others, and in so doing, to develop His character within ourselves. But allowing choice means human beings are allowed to cause others suffering and pain. Indeed, most suffering is caused by human choices, and very little by events such as natural disasters.

Third, people say to me as a doctor that if God were a good God, there would not be so much illness. My reply is very different. I am astonished that we experience so much good health. Every day you and I experience a hundred thousand minor miracles inside our own bodies. The more I study the workings of a single cell, and the body as a whole, the greater the daily miracles appear to be. If only cars or computers were as reliable and as self-repairing as our own bodies are.

Fourth, people say that it's not fair that some have an easy life and some a hard – or a short – life. But that is to limit our perspective only to the time-space world, when we know the truth that one day all this will fall away, that death itself is but a gateway from a very limited kind of existence to a new dimension in eternity forever. We know that we will be judged by what we have received and much will be expected from those to whom much has been given. We know from the story of the rich man and Lazarus that we will be called to account, and that God, who is the one who knows all and sees all, also is a just God. Who are we to say that a child has 'missed out' because it began to experience eternal life at the age of four rather than the age of eighty-four?

Paul tells us that to live is Christ, but to die is gain. The secret of being a disciple is knowing how to be content, fulfilled and at peace in every circumstance: in sickness and health, in richness and extreme poverty, in what appears to be success and in what is written off by others as failure, in personal triumphs and in darkest disasters.

But these are mere words. It's one thing to agree in our heads, another to work it all out when confronted with the daily realities and grind of life. That is what this book is about, and why what follows could well turn out to be the most important book – apart from the Bible itself – that you have ever read.

Dr Patrick Dixon
October 2001

Acknowledgements

First I want to acknowledge the presence of Jesus that my family and I experienced during some of the times that are mentioned in this book. Without God's faithfulness in a very real and practical way, this story would not be ending in the way that it is.

Second I want to affirm my son Justyn, who has allowed his story to be written and has contributed his own pages to this book which tell his side of the story. In the end, his courage and determination are very clear. Despite all his difficulties, Justyn achieved four As at A level, and is now doing further Christian training as preparation for university.

I also want to give thanks to my friend Ila who has put hundreds of hours into typing as I have dictated and has been my friend and confidante throughout this experience. And also to Andrew Wooding, who as always takes my limited English and works his wonders.

And to my editor, David, who heard me preach on this subject and took the brave decision to commission this book. Many thanks.

Finally I want to give thanks to the three wonderful women in my life, my wife Ailish and my daughters Kiera and Laura, who bring with them, wherever they go, sunshine and fun.

Introduction

It is no good sweeping pain under the carpet. Pain is a living reality that in one way or another most of you will face – whether the pain of the death of a loved one, sickness in your life or those close to you, or a trauma that you or any member of your family may face. For most, it is not a question of 'if' you face one of these difficulties, it is when.

My hope is that through this book you will gain fresh insight into God's provision for helping you go through life's difficulties and emerge with your faith intact or even stronger. If you have been damaged, you can find the pathway back. Just survival would be good, too!

It is also the purpose of this book to look at disillusionment, the first cousin to pain. Disillusionment is a lot more insidious in the way that it operates. While pain is often sudden and traumatic, coming into our lives very quickly and profoundly, disillusionment is like a cancer that can destroy your spiritual soul, shattering your hope and faith over a period of years. There are no magic solutions, but you *can* find purposeful and practical pathways through the disillusionment.

I have taken the liberty of telling something of my family's story in the first chapter of this book, and coming back to it in later chapters. This book has not been written from a distant, theoretical position. In some measure, it has come out of the pain and difficulty that I myself have faced.

I hope and pray that the story I tell and the biblical principles we look at will help us all.

1

It's All Right to Feel Pain –
A Personal Story

Back in February 1995 you would have thought that the Singlehurst family was happy. It consisted (and still does!) of myself, my wife Ailish, and our three children, Kiera, Justyn and Laura.

I was the director of Youth With A Mission, England. Also known as YWAM, it is a relatively successful missionary organisation and a respected spiritual ministry. I had a happy marriage and three great children. On the outside, all looked well.

But slowly brewing in the life of our son Justyn was a time bomb that was about to explode. The explosion would be catastrophic, causing much pain and heartbreak. Its intensity would last for about two years, and its impact would continue for a few more.

Blow-up day arrived on 11 March 1995, which happened to be my birthday. Justyn, who was thirteen at the time, had always been different from the two girls, not just in that he was a boy, but in the amount of energy and hyper-activity that was evident in all that he did. While to others he might have looked like a slightly out-of-control enthusiastic adolescent, he was to us our own very special son.

No one had prepared us for a day like this, full of emotional storms. Like all storms, it started with a squall that we hoped would pass. But the squall developed into a raging tornado that would cruelly snatch our lives up and spin us around. It would shake our every foundation, and all the faith that we as a family could muster. It would stretch every relationship we had, and would test the very fabric of our marriage and our commitment to Jesus.

It all began with an argument while walking along a street, a disagreement between Justyn and me. It caused him to say things that I had never heard from him before.

'Dad, you don't love me.'

'Why not?' I said, taken aback by the candidness of his comment.

'If you love me, how come you spend twelve weeks a year travelling? You've missed over four years of my life. I hate you.'

My birthday joy faded away. *Well, it's just a conversation*, I thought. *It will be gone soon.* But by the evening Justyn was locked in the toilet screaming hate and abuse at me.

'I hate you! I hate you! I hate you!'

He was by this time so beside himself that in desperation I asked a youth worker[1] connected with YWAM to come and talk to him. The youth worker suggested that Justyn go and stay the night with him, which we readily agreed to, thinking it would be for the best.

But it wasn't. The next day, when we picked Justyn up, his attitude was even more aggressive and truculent. In talking to him later, we discovered that this youth worker had some major problems in his life. He had used this opportunity not to help Justyn but to make matters worse. Justyn had been feeling a little bit guilty about his anger that day, but this youth worker confirmed to Justyn that his anger was fine, that in fact I *didn't* love him and that I had in effect left him. This legitimising of his anger only intensified its ferocity.

Justyn no longer wanted to go to school. He had just changed from a Christian school in Harpenden, Hertfordshire, that specialised in individual learning, to a large comprehensive which had a Christian heritage. It was a change that he himself had wanted, but in practical terms he had gone from being one of a hundred children to one of twelve hundred. What we later found out was that this exacerbated Justyn's underlying learning difficulty as he no longer had such individual attention from teachers.

As the days raged on, the squall grew moment by moment in intensity. I tried to talk to Justyn about why I travelled. As a family, we had previously been happy with my missionary work and the good times we had spent together. But it was as if these good times had never existed. Justyn's only cry was still, 'I hate you!'

His behaviour gradually deteriorated. Every day it became more difficult, more abusive, even violent. We spoke to a psychologist friend. He tried to reassure us, saying, 'It will be fine. It will go away.' But it didn't.

Justyn had always been hyperactive, but in the end he had always done as he was told. Now he wouldn't do anything. He began to disappear. He'd run out of the house, screaming, in the evenings. We wouldn't know where he was. Tearful hours were spent searching Harpenden for him.

He would run out of the house and I would chase him down the hill, calling and calling. But he was too fast for me and he'd be gone.

As the intensity grew, the violence began to spill over at school. A sharp compass was jabbed into another boy for no apparent reason. There were phone calls from concerned teachers. Week by week, Justyn became more and more out of control.

He had never really sworn before, but suddenly we had a new resident in our house. It was most unwelcome – the 'f' word. We had prided ourselves on being a good Christian family and didn't like that 'f' word very much, particularly as it seemed to punctuate every sentence. It was the adjective that described every noun.

It was more than the 'f' word, though. This young thirteen-year-old was bringing his violence and aggression home. It was deeply disturbing to Ailish and Justyn's sisters, but the aggression was largely directed towards me. It wasn't long before Justyn took a good swing at me – and connected.

By this time we were trying every remedy under the sun: anger, praying, shouting, and any other disciplinary measure we could think of. Some days, it would appear as if answers were coming and the storm had lulled. In reality, though, it had only lulled to later intensify.

My mobile phone would ring often as other YWAM staff who lived in the community phoned to say that Justyn had called them an 'f***ing this and that' and what was I going to do about it? Or Justyn had hit one of their children and what was I going to do about it? Justyn had done this and Justyn had said that, and *what was I going to do about it?*

Not only was Justyn's control slipping away, so was ours.

I sat one day in the car, thinking, as I was about to lead a meeting on training and equipping people for youth work, *How can I do this? My own son is totally and absolutely out of control.* The tears began to flow. I sank to the floor of the car crying, 'Oh, God.'

Little did we know that things were about to take a dramatic turn for the worse.

One morning, Justyn came down to our kitchen with a strange look on his face.

'I've just swallowed a bottle of paracetamol,' he announced calmly. We raced upstairs, and sure enough, there was the bottle. The label said it contained fifty tablets, but now it was empty. *Oh, God.*

The phone call, the rush to the hospital, and Justyn was taken behind the curtain. A few moments later, a doctor appeared, looking grave.

'If he's taken forty pills or more, he will probably die,' the doctor explained. 'If he's taken twenty or less, it should be fine. Anywhere in between, he could have severe liver damage. We've given him medicine to be sick. Now we'll take him into hospital to observe him.'

We had thought before that things were as bad as they could be, but now the bottom of our world had completely disappeared. All Ailish and I could do was sit and cry.

'How could this happen to us? We're nice Christian people. We've done our best. This is meant to happen to people out there, not us. Where *are* you, God? Where did you go?'

Thus began a very long day. A day of Justyn throwing up. A day of his blood being analysed. A day of waiting, and waiting, and waiting.

Finally, another doctor appeared. He told us, 'You're very fortunate people. We estimate that your son took around twenty tablets. But since he told you only minutes afterwards, and as we've made him throw them up, there will be very little damage.'

That sounded like good news. *Great* news. But the doctor went on to say, 'However, Justyn will have to remain in hospital for a full psychiatric assessment. And of course, he will have to be referred to Social Services.'

Somehow life went on in the next few days. I'd preach at churches, lead YWAM meetings, fulfil other responsibilities, but it was all unreal, as if I was living someone else's life. Our family's existence centred on a hospital bed, waiting for a psychiatrist. Whenever Justyn was interviewed, all he could tell people was how much he hated me.

Eventually, I sat in a room with a psychiatrist and Justyn. Justyn told of how he felt he had been deserted by me, and how I didn't love him. I could see the psychiatrist's face. I could imagine his thoughts.

As the psychiatrist conducted the interview, it began to dawn on me that another possibility might be running through his mind: that I had abused Justyn in some way or other. The more Justyn talked, the more awful things sounded. Then another thought hit me: *What if they take him away?*

On a side note, I asked the psychiatrist later if he had initially suspected abuse, and he said, 'Yes.' He had, however, soon ruled this out as a result of Justyn's body language and some of the things he had said. Four days later we were allowed to take him home.

But there was more violence, more aggression against

Kiera and Laura, and continuing disturbance at the Oval, the YWAM community that we lived in. This included other children getting black eyes after fisticuffs with Justyn. And there were still more calls on my mobile phone, like the time I was in Sainsbury's and a very irate senior YWAM leader called. I was informed in angry tones that Justyn had told him to 'f*** off'. *What was I going to do about it?*

At this point we were referred to Social Services and a specialised unit in St Albans that looks at dysfunctional families. This stirred a number of emotions in Ailish and me. We felt tremendous guilt and shame at our own failure. Then we were afraid that Social Services might want to blame us and take Justyn away. Our crisis and pain had reached its pinnacle. Life was becoming unliveable.

Ailish and I went for our first visit to the specialised unit in St Albans under a cloud of foreboding. Would they think they were looking at abusive parents? What would be going on in their minds?

To our relief and surprise, the people we met were very straightforward and pleasant. They gently told us that our family was out of control and it was their job to help us to regain control. We were the parents – we should have positive control of our family. We clearly did not, and Justyn was in many ways controlling the entire family. This needed to stop, and they would seek to help us.

So began a year of intense meetings where we were probed and quizzed to find out what was really going on. Once, the whole family had a meeting that was observed through two-way mirrors. What an awful meeting that was – Justyn out of control, screams, tears, hurtful accusations.

As a result of these meetings, the specialists soon put their finger on a major dysfunction that Ailish and I had in parenting. Ailish is a person of principle. If she says something, she means it. If she draws a line and says there will be consequences, there *will* be. She sees problems early on. She deals with little things because she knows that they will grow into big things.

I, on the other hand, am Mr Abstract. Words are just words. They're meaningful the moment they come out of my mouth, but from then on they are negotiable. I am very tolerant, so the early warning signs are never heeded. My tolerance overcomes the initial irritation of wrong behaviour. Unfortunately, though, when the behaviour does not change, my tolerance eventually explodes into anger.

These two approaches weren't compatible. Every time Ailish sought to bring control, my tolerance undermined it. Every time I said there would be consequences, I didn't give them. Even more fundamental than that, while Ailish was genuinely angry at the bad side of Justyn's behaviour – at the way he treated his sisters, and how he wreaked havoc – I somehow just wanted to make the whole thing right again. There was no underlying righteous anger.

I was horrified when the specialists recommended that I seek professional help. Here was the ultimate humiliation. Spring Harvest speaker. Director of YWAM England. One of the organisers behind March for Jesus. Now I would have to do two things: realise that I had a problem, then go and see a psychologist.

Sitting in the consulting room of a psychologist, answering all his questions, is a very strange experience. I couldn't help wondering exactly what he thought and where it was all leading.

After about five sessions, the psychologist said to me, 'Mr Singlehurst, you are suffering from what I will call "the Harrods syndrome".'

The psychologist had asked a lot of questions that related not only to Justyn and our current family situation, but also my own childhood. He had taken me through some of the dysfunction of my own family – a family where I had a wonderful father, but a father who was in some areas very dysfunctional. He was something of a Jekyll and Hyde personality: a man of great compassion and tenderness, and tremendous intellectual understanding, but who in a split second could turn into a man of great violence and uncontrollable anger. To compensate, my equally wonderful mother, whenever there was pain in the household, would take me to Harrods.

It was at Harrods where, as a little boy, I would be treated to a meal in the restaurant at the top of the building, and would have a day of wonderful unreality where my mother would shine for my benefit. She was the star who would help me feel good feelings and think good thoughts. What this did, though, was build into me a tendency to avoid confrontation and difficult situations. If I heard anybody shout, if there were voices raised, it would literally make me feel physically ill. Confrontation was to be avoided at all costs.

My psychologist pointed out to me that the reactions I had had to my son, which I used in a sense to overrule Ailish's judgements, were not as wonderfully Christian and tolerant as I had thought. My responses were entirely wrong and were founded largely on my own background. Every time Justyn misbehaved, instead of drawing boundaries, being righteously angry and being in control, I was trying to 'take him to Harrods', trying to create happy families. To put it bluntly, I was avoiding the problem.

Furthermore, the psychologist graciously pointed out to me that over many years I had been undermining my wife, putting down her opinions and making her feel bad about her responses and reactions. As it turned out, she had been right and I had been wrong.

This was the final humiliation for me. There was the awful sense that not only had I failed as a father, I had also failed as a husband. The emotional quicksand was getting deeper and deeper. How would I ever pull myself out of this gloom and deep darkness?

After this particular session, I sat in the car with tears pouring down my face. I cried out to God, 'Lord, can you help? Where are you just at this moment? Where do we go from here?'

The Singlehurst family entered a two-year period of intense pain and difficulty. In the midst of Justyn's anger and lashing out, he turned to us one day and claimed that a male Christian worker had been making advances towards him and had put his hand up Justyn's jumper. In our minds, Justyn had become unreliable and was making wild accusations about people. We ignored his outcry and told him not to be so stupid. But we were wrong.

Our psychologist friend had initially thought Justyn's problem would go away quite quickly. He was puzzled as to why Justyn was so angry. So were we, and our answer came a year later.

By this time, we had made some progress in helping Justyn. We had discovered that the Christian worker he mentioned was a paedophile. It was the worker Justyn had stayed with the first night of his anger.

He had indeed tried to seduce Justyn, and part of his strategy had been to tell Justyn that if I really loved him, I wouldn't have travelled as much or done the things I'd done. This had obviously fuelled Justyn's anger and intensified the problem.

Fortunately, Justyn had resisted this man's advances and had tried to inform us of the danger. Our rejection of his warning only compounded his anger. This could not be dealt with until we discovered the horrible truth some time later.

Nine months into the problem we realised the other reason for Justyn's difficulties. He was suffering from Attention Deficit Hyperactivity Disorder – in other words, he was an ADHD kid.[2] While he was in his nice Christian school, with an approach to education that was based on individual learning, this did not manifest itself in such a strong way. However, when Justyn transferred to a large comprehensive school and was in an open system, he couldn't concentrate and felt totally at sea.

All of Justyn's problems manifested at the same time, causing the severity of the situation.

As I will describe later on, we were fortunate to find some answers – through personal change, through answered prayer, through medical and psychological assistance, and through the help of friends, church members and leaders.

We discovered that there was life beyond the clouds.

Justyn's own story

You will be pleased to know that Justyn is alive and well. The first appendix at the back of the book is a chapter by Justyn where he tells his side of the story, and what was going on in his life during the years I've mentioned in this chapter.

2

Jesus – His Pain and Disillusionment

One of the prayers I am sure we have all prayed, and perhaps even *screamed* at God, is: 'What do you know about pain and suffering? Don't you know what it's like down here?'

We may have a picture in our minds of a sheltered God in a wonderful heaven filled with joy and peace – a God who says he is love, yet has no real conception of pain, suffering or difficulty. This accusation not only rings true in our own hearts, but we hear it in the world out there. Yet it is totally unfounded.

John 3:16 is the most famous verse in the New Testament:

> For God so loved the world that he gave his one and only Son, that whoever believes in him shall not perish but have eternal life.

These words describe the type of love that God has for us. God is not far removed from our sufferings, and not unsympathetic to the difficulties. He has in fact taken the bad track. He has been there already, experiencing the worst types of pain and disillusionment.

Let us look at the life of Jesus and see something of the

journey that he took – the journey that God in human flesh made in identifying with the world.

What do we know about Jesus? First of all, he was born into an occupied nation with a puppet government that took its orders from Rome.

I suspect that most people reading this book will have no understanding of what it means to live in an occupied country, but we all know stories of occupied European nations in the Second World War. We will also be aware of the recent history of the Eastern Bloc countries that were under Soviet control. Those born in occupied countries live with fear, oppression, a lack of identity and the sense that their culture is being twisted – that their freedom and capacity to express themselves in their own language are being robbed.

You may have seen the Hollywood blockbuster *Braveheart*. In this film, William Wallace found himself in similar circumstances. He experienced the pain of his country being controlled by another nation, and he longed for freedom.

God in heaven fully understands what it means to be born in the wrong nation at the wrong time. Worse than this, Jesus was raised in Galilee. At that time the people of Galilee were looked down on. Not only was he born in an occupied nation – a very small and forgotten nation at that – he was also born in the wrong part.

It is a sad fact that all over the world we have stratified our cultures. Humans take great delight in saying that some places are better to come from than others. Many people struggle their whole lives because, through no fault of their own, they were born in a place of little opportunity – the wrong side of town. They are less likely to enjoy a good education and it is often harder for them to reach their potential.

What does God know about this? He understands fully, because *he* came from the wrong part of town.

We can assume that for most of Jesus' life, people would have wondered and had questions about his conception and birth. Those in his town knew that Joseph wasn't married to Mary at the time of conception. These rumours and questions would have circulated and reflected not only on Jesus, but also on his mother and her reputation.

One of the most difficult types of pain to deal with is the sense of being unwanted, of having your very identity questioned: 'Who are you?' Of being looked down on because your skin is a different colour, for instance.

How many have suffered in playgrounds, have seen the look of unacceptance in people's eyes, have experienced the questions – have felt rejected before life really began? How many have lived under the curse of feeling second or even third class?

What can God know about this? He knows an awful lot. He's been there. Seen the sneers. Heard the whispers. Experienced the pain.

On top of all this, Jesus experienced being a refugee. He spent the first few years of his life not in his own nation but as a political refugee, fleeing for his very life as the government of the day were looking for this boy king, this Prince of Peace. Herod had heard the stories and met the wise men. He did not want any other potential kings to be growing up in his land. So Jesus was taken to Egypt.

In this century right now, there are millions of refugees all around the world. These are people who, for one reason or another (war, political corruption, their tribe or back-ground), have had to flee. They can't grow up where they want to grow up. They become squatters in other nations, the lowest of the low.

For many, being a refugee means that you are at the bottom end of the pecking order – there is nowhere else to go. You live as a fearful, temporary resident, taking whatever crumbs of hospitality and opportunity are open to you.

You must have seen the footage of the refugee sites on television news reports. If you looked closely, you would have seen the pain on the refugees' faces. If you listened carefully, you would have heard their sobbing children. They are people divorced from their culture. People who are lost. They are lonely individuals in someone else's world.

Sounds like hell on earth. Can God understand this? Does he know the pain of these people? Yes, Jesus has been there. God in the flesh has already experienced it. He knows.

Jesus wasn't born into a family of influence and promi-nence. Instead, he came from a poor family. Kings are from the finest backgrounds, princes from the richest families, and rulers from places of power. It is not often, even today, that the world changers, the world shakers, come from among the poor.

There is never quite enough in a poor family. Children are fed but always hungry. Clothes are there but always well worn. Grinding poverty ages people prematurely and robs them of their dignity. There is no freedom and little enjoy-ment in the day-to-day battle to make do. Many of us would have loved to have come from the better families, the better backgrounds. If only . . .

What does God know about poverty and its impact on

people's lives? What does he know about coming from a poor family? He knows *all* about it. Jesus came from just such a background.

Jesus not only understood the suffering that happens just because it happens, he also created environments of his own choice which opened up a whole new dimension to pain and suffering.

Do you fancy the idea of your life message being so extreme, so challenging, that you will be totally misunderstood and persecuted? Do you fancy having a message that includes such radical statements as 'I am the way, the truth and the life'? Or describing the influential people of the day as 'white-washed sepulchres'?

Of having a message that meant you broke all the social norms of your day? You touched the lepers, and you had women on your team when some said it was better to be born a dog than a woman. You made friends with those most despised.

You said that you were God, and there was a new way to live – that people could find the love of God, and his love would transform them. What you speak about is not what can be seen or understood in the real world, but alludes to another world, a spiritual world.

Most historians and politicians would say – even Jesus' enemies would say – that he was the carrier of one of the most radical, even disturbing, messages that the world has ever seen.

Many in our world have known the difficulty of bearing a message that is hard for people to receive. They have tried to articulate something that people don't understand, and have often been persecuted for it. Think of Galileo, Wycliffe or, for that matter, Karl Marx. Nelson Mandela spent twenty years locked up because of his cry for freedom.

Does God understand what it means to have a vision that no one understands – a message that leads to persecution? The answer, of course, is yes. Jesus has already been there. He's carried the story, spread the message and lived out the consequences.

Inside most of us is the pain of relationships gone wrong, of expectations not met. The pain that comes when our friends, the people we trust the most, have in some way betrayed us or let us down. Once again we might ask the question, 'What does God know about this? How can Jesus understand how we feel?'

When we look at the life of Jesus, we can see very clearly that he experienced rejection, false accusation and, in the end, the worst type of betrayal from the religious leaders, the ordinary people, and ultimately from his closest and dearest disciples.

Perhaps you can picture Jesus in the garden at Gethsemane. He is feeling the burden of what is about to take place, knowing that very soon he will be giving up his life in the most horrendous way possible. He asks his friends to wait, to pray, to be with him. But in the midst of his vulnerability, his fair-weather friends fall asleep. They are so used to Jesus meeting their own needs and being there for *them* that in this one moment when he wants them to be there for *him*, they can't do it. They are more interested in their own physical needs.

Then, for the sake of thirty silver coins, Judas, who has been with Jesus from the beginning, is going to lead the temple guards to Jesus to have him arrested.

Can you imagine what it means to pour your life into somebody, to give him or her everything you have, yet in the end they stab you in the back? Jesus has been there. He knows what it feels like.

But it gets worse. Judas was *one* of the disciples, but Peter was among the three most important. He was as close to Jesus as a person could be. He was the chosen successor, the leader in the group, the key man. Peter was all of Jesus' aspirations for the future. Jesus' dream for the Church rested on this small team and in particular on Peter.

But Jesus already knew what was going to happen when he told Peter: 'You will betray me. You will deny me.'

Peter spoke out loudly, 'Not me.' But just as Jesus said it would be, it was.

You and I have experienced relational pain, and will experience it again. Does Jesus understand? Has he been there? Of course he's been there.

The greatest pain a human can experience is slow, protracted torture that leads to death. The greatest pain that a pure and wonderful God can experience is to have his purity marred and spoiled by the sin and selfishness of mankind.

There can be no darker cry that has ever gone up from planet earth than that which came from the mouth of Jesus on the cross: 'My God, my God, why have you forsaken me?'

Can you even begin to imagine the journey that Jesus had been on that day? Being dressed up in fine clothes and mocked. A crown of thorns pressed down on to his head. The beating and the scourging. Being pushed into the street to carry the crossbeam. Stumbling along, dirty and naked, while mocked by the crowds.

21

Finally, being strapped to the cross. The sound of nails ringing on the hammer. The slow lifting of the cross, then the shuddering, dislocating, joint-wrenching agony as it thunders into the hole in the ground. Pain like that is hard to imagine. The stares. The pointing.

In a sense, Jesus allowed all of this to happen. This was not imposed upon him. His own free choice had taken him this way.

There is more than physical pain here – it is a pain that we cannot understand. The Bible doesn't say much about it, but it does imply the deep theological truth that the sin and suffering of the world was placed upon Christ at that time.

The unity of the Godhead – Father, Son and Holy Spirit, the incredible three in one – had been together since the very beginning, before all time. But purity and holiness were about to be shattered. Jesus was going to be ripped out of the Trinity and separated for a moment in time.

Just as the Bible tells us that physical darkness came upon the face of the earth, darkness must have also come into the heart of God. Certainly it came into the heart of Jesus. This is pain that is hard to describe or even think about, with holiness defiled in such an appalling way.

Think about it. When you experience your pain, your hurts, your disillusionment, you might ask yourself: 'Does God understand? Can he know what I'm going through?'

Surely if we listen carefully, we will hear the whisper that echoes across human history: 'Yes, I understand. I've been there too, my friend.'

3

Pain – Where Does It Come From?

Here is a simple truth: there is no avoiding pain. It is part of being human, part of living in this world of ours. Pain is not something to be avoided; rather, it is something to be prepared for.

It is not really the purpose of this book to examine in great detail where pain comes from. Finer minds than mine have produced many worthy words on this subject. This book has been written to give practical help on dealing with pain and working through it. Nevertheless, here are a few brief observations.

Does pain come from God? Could God not have created us in such a way that we were pain-free? This is one of the most commonly asked questions, and of course one of the most common accusations against God is that God should have created the world in such a way that there was no pain or problems. I've no doubt that this could have been possible. But the only problem is that the world would not have been inhabited by us, but rather by some form of controlled or mechanical beings.

Innate in humankind is our freedom. We are not beings that are controlled by instinct or environment, but have the capacity to determine our own behaviour. Obviously this is

influenced by background and other factors, but not determined.

Therefore, because we are free, we have had historically,
and always will have in the future, the capacity to cause
tremendous pain to each other. God cannot limit our
capacity to do this by direct action in terms of freezing our
will, because that would be arbitrary, and it would turn us
into controlled beings. But rather, Christians would argue,
God has sought to influence the world and show us that we
can live in another way. Ultimately, through the sacrifice of
Christ, he has given us a pathway to God and guidelines on
how to live under the principles that would limit our
capacity to do damage.

Most of the pain that the world faces, that you and I
face, is caused by humans in one way or another – maybe
through institutions we have created, the selfishness of our
individual or corporate lifestyles, or the deliberate or sometimes accidental way we treat one another.

It is certainly in the heart of God to limit the amount of
pain in the world. In the book of Genesis we read the story
of two trees in the Garden of Eden: one, the tree of life; the
other, the tree of the knowledge of good and evil. These two
trees symbolise the choices that we as humans make, both
individually and corporately.

If you live under the principles of the tree of life – in
other words, under God's definition of what is right and
wrong – you will limit the effects of your selfishness and the
pain that you cause, because Christians believe that God
created the world and everything in it (Psalm 24:1). God
created humankind, and as the creator, God knows what is
the right way for us to live, and what is the wrong way for

us to live. Therefore God's laws and guidelines are not some arbitrary list to stop our fun, but rather are the principles and guidelines that stop us from damaging ourselves and others. The tree of life was the symbol of our relationship with God and it was God's hope that we would put him in the centre of our universe, and that through relationship with God we would live under his principles.

The tree of the knowledge of good and evil symbolises the second option for humankind. That is that we would place ourselves at the centre of the universe and, either corporately or individually, we would choose for ourselves what is good and evil, and what is right and wrong.

The appalling flaw of this is that because we are not the designers, we actually are very unsure of what is good and evil, right and wrong. Different cultures, different religions end up with a different understanding. It becomes arbitrary, and so we open up for ourselves a Pandora's box of problems. While it is true that, as humans, we are capable of acts of great goodness, great kindness and self-sacrifice, we are also capable of selfishness, both on an appalling scale and also insidious little acts of selfishness, which in themselves have deep consequences on the lives of others. Worse still, we are often confused about what is right and wrong, and do wrong in the name of right and cause yet more problems.

With the Ten Commandments, God has given us a standard from heaven, a guideline for humans that will limit pain. If people live inside the principles of the Ten Commandments, they will cause a lot less pain in the world than if they live outside them.

In other words, the commandments are the summary of God's value system. These values, as summarised in the commandments, are there to protect you and to guide you and to show you the right way to live. These values highlight a number of different things.

First is the value of God. When you accept God's value, obviously this has an impact on you, inasmuch as it gives the opportunity for you to live for someone who has more value than yourself. It reminds you that God is at the centre of the universe and also that there is a judge at the centre of the universe, and therefore one day accountability. When you live as if there is no God and humankind is at the centre of the universe, then somehow love fades away. You begin to live as if there are no consequences to your wrongdoing, and you can then see the pain that comes from this. When you live as if there is a God of love at the centre of the universe, and he is a judge, then actually that does impact your behaviour, and the world is hopefully a better place.

Second, the Ten Commandments give huge value to people, to human life: 'thou shall not kill'. This incredible value that God places on human life is therefore meant to affect our behaviour, so that we treat each other with love, kindness and dignity. All around the world, you can see what happens when we ignore this value and command. Murder, the devaluing of human life, starvation that is caused because we don't share our food resources, and all manner of appalling actions happen when we do not place value on human life. If we did value life in the same way that God does and treated each other accordingly, the world would be a different place.

A third value is the value of relationships: 'do not commit adultery', 'honour your father and mother' – all of this relates to the importance God places in relationships. Life is much better when you honour the relationships that you have, and when you try wherever possible to live in harmony with one another and respect these two very important relationships of husband to wife and children to parents. But, of course, the principle goes beyond those to every kind of relationship.

The fourth area is the value that God places on the possessions and belongings of other people: 'do not covet', 'do not steal'. Obviously, as you look around the world today, a great part of our problems and our pain is caused by the fact that we do steal, we do covet, and God wants us to respect the possessions of others.

The fifth value that comes across here is that we should respect ourselves. 'Keep the Sabbath holy' is about the way you look after yourself. You need rest. We as human beings are intrinsically valuable. Again, you see the tremendous problems that are caused in our world by poor self-image, by the stress and abuse that we bring upon ourselves. Again, the world would be a better place if we valued ourselves more highly.

Of course, Christians believe that God's ultimate plan to deal with the pain caused by human freedom is Jesus. In 2 Corinthians 5:15, the Apostle Paul outlines the core message of the gospel: instead of living for ourselves we should now live for Christ.

Through our relationship with God in Christ we can be enabled to live under the principles of the tree of life. Through Christ and the power of the Holy Spirit, we don't choose for ourselves what is right and wrong. Instead, we are to submit to the principles of scripture and the Christian faith.

Even though pain does not come from God, God does allow the possibility of it, and also created the consequences of wrongdoing. C. S. Lewis argued in his book *The Problem of Pain* that in one sense pain is a gift from God – this is because it often tells us that we have walked away from God and are where we ought not to be.

There is no doubt in my mind that God is as grieved by pain and selfishness as we are. With much of the pain in this world, God has done all that can be done without freezing our freedom. God has sought by conscience, by law, by the death and resurrection of Jesus, and by the Holy Spirit, to steer us away from those things that cause so much pain.

Of course, there are different types of pain: physical pain, and death because our human duration is limited, and emotional pain. Wherever we face any of these it will cause many reactions such as physical pain, fear and emotional disturbance.

You may already know what it is like to be in a hospital room and see a loved one die. To experience the awful finality, the heart-shattering loss, the many questions of why, particularly if the loved one died prematurely in unexpected and difficult circumstances. Even when you know someone will die because of old age or sickness, you will still not be prepared. You will still feel pain.

A good friend of mine has the worst kind of multiple sclerosis. In just a few years, her illness has taken her from being the life and soul of the party to someone who is forced to be housebound. She is living her life as best she can from a wheelchair. Imagine her pain – and the pain of her husband as, day by day, he wakes up and finds that in one sense there is a little bit less of his wife than there was when he went to bed. This is real pain.

Pain isn't just tied up with our physical frailty. It also comes from horrendous things that humans do to one another. Every one of us, throughout the world, has been a victim of human selfishness to one degree or another. Human beings have an incredible capacity to damage and hurt each other, whether through war, famine, the selfishness of a dysfunctional relationship, marital abuse, the neglect of a child, the careless words that we can so easily speak, or thousands of other ways.

Here is an example that shows just how a few seemingly harmless words can unfortunately have a major impact on another person's life. I once knew someone who couldn't make decisions. This was because he had always been compared to his attractive, dynamic sister. This doesn't sound like much of a problem until you realise that for him getting dressed could take all day. He would put on a set of clothes, then immediately be overwhelmed with doubt and confusion about whether they were the right ones, or if he would look more attractive in other clothes. So he would take them off and put on another set. Then another. And another.

You could be the victim of corporate selfishness. You might come back from holiday and find that your company has made you redundant. Suddenly, without warning, you have been dumped on the scrap heap of life, or so it would seem. You are a victim of corporate strategy, of downsizing because oil prices went up, currency went down, or your company just doesn't need you any more.

Your pain might also be caused by yourself. You can

make choices that might initially seem innocent and even beneficial, but ultimately cause harm.

Perhaps you are experiencing some of the miseries of life, and you choose a certain drug that appears to offer peace and freedom. Not only does this drug not cover up the pain that caused you to take it in the first place, it now causes far more extra pain than you could ever have imagined. This, of course, also includes alcohol abuse.

There are many ways that running away from pain can create more pain. A marriage is in difficulty. A relationship seems to be bankrupt, so one of the partners secretly gets involved in another relationship. A sexual need that is not being met in one relationship is satisfied elsewhere, but instead of solving the pain of the first dysfunctional relationship, more pain is created. In looking for an easy way out, things only become worse.

It would be nice if you could blame somebody for this sort of pain, be it God, or this or that. But the only person you can blame is yourself.

Can pain sometimes be positive? I think it can. Some of the greatest acts of human courage, human goodness and human sacrifice have been the result of some sort of pain. Pain can help you grow. It shows you what is of real value. It can even reveal what is weak in your own character.

When I saw my father die at a relatively early age, relationships suddenly became very important. This sort of pain can speak to you and educate you. It tells you that you need to make the most of today. Don't put off till tomorrow getting that relationship right, or getting to know a certain person better. The sad fact is that there may not be a tomorrow.

We have now had a brief look at the causes of pain. What I mainly want to do in this book is seek to find ways that Christians can deal with pain, wherever it comes from.

Does God have a pathway for you? Does he care? Can you find help?

Is there really a way out?

4

Disillusionment –

Where Does It Come From?

The difference between pain and disillusionment can be described like this: if pain is finding yourself in the grip of a fast-acting heart attack, disillusionment is more like a slow cancer eating away at your soul over a long period of time.

Its impact causes a cloud to come between you and your dreams. If you are a Christian, it might even be that a cloud comes between you and your relationship with the Son. You know disillusionment has a grip on your life when you can only describe your future in terms of the cloud. Hope has disappeared, and you can no longer talk about the dream or vision that is beyond the clouds.

The essence of Christianity is that we are people destined to live beyond the clouds. We may not see in our own lives all that we dream of, but we still need to live in that dream.

The poet Edwin Markham once said:

> Great it is to believe the dream
> When we stand in youth by the starry stream;
> But a greater thing is to fight life through
> And say at the end, 'the dream is true'.[3]

This is the test for each one of us, to end our days as the poet describes: not living our life in the gloom of the cloud, but living in the reality of the dream.

It is disturbing to me to see so many Christians, of many years' standing, who while going through the motions of their Christian faith are definitely living in their disillusionment. This disillusionment shapes their decisions.

In recent years, as I have gone round many, many churches I have found mature Christians describing leaders that they once loved and trusted in rather disillusioned terms. You can see that they have a great deal of concern about their leader, and in a sense they can no longer see the strengths of this person, but are more impacted by their weaknesses.

The same is true about church in general. There is no doubt that, with all that is happening in the world, this is a challenging time for the Church, and it is very common to hear people speaking about their local church in far from positive tones.

Let us look closely at five areas that can cause disillusionment, particularly in the Christian life.

Church

The Church is a wonderful gathering of God's people that gives each Christian fellowship, encouragement, a vision for life, and leadership enabling us to fulfil the commandments that Jesus gives: to love God, to love each other, and to be salt and light in this world. This is what the Church is . . . or rather, is meant to be.

Unfortunately, many people's experience is that their

church does not fulfil these aspirations. They might be attending a church that is not very spiritually alive, and they are finding little encouragement in their Christian lives. But in 'lively' churches there are just as many people, if not more, who are also disillusioned.

For some Christians, disillusionment is caused by '*under*-promise'. They are desperate for spiritual life and encouragement, yet the structure they are in is dry, religious, cold and unfriendly. They feel alone, neither encouraged nor supported. Slowly but surely, the clouds grow darker, and they feel unable to aspire to the dream.

Others suffer from '*over*-promise'. They are in churches where everything is promised in terms of spiritual blessing, pastoring, encouragement, vision and direction, yet ultimately nothing is delivered. There is a continual dream placed before them, but there is no practical reality. There is an illusion of friendliness, but no real community. There is an enthusiastic spirituality, but depth is hard to come by. There is talk of taking the world for Christ, but people are struggling to reach the neighbourhood around them.

Whether you're in a church that suffers from 'under-promise' or 'over-promise', this wonderful God-given institution is unfortunately helping to build your disillusionment instead of helping you reach your dream and live in the light of the Son.

Christian leadership

Another cause of disillusionment is the way Christian leaders interact with people. I'm a Christian leader, so I don't want to be judgmental, and I do believe the Church needs good, empowering Christian leaders. But I also want to be honest and recognise that Christian leaders have often acted in ways that cause hurt and disillusionment. This is not because they are making a conscious choice to be bad leaders. It is because they are the fruit of their training and their character weaknesses, or lack practical and honest systems of accountability which could help them lead differently.

The over-enthusiastic leader

There are different types of Christian leader. One is the over-enthusiastic leader. He or she hears from God, and out of their personal conviction that God has spoken to them, shares their vision. Unfortunately, it is often shared in such a way that there is no opportunity for the ordinary church member to have ownership, and the person who doesn't come on board with the vision is made to feel like a spiritual rebel. Everything else you feel God has said to you has to be subservient to this new strong vision that the leader has. All other visions go by the wayside.

This kind of leader often talks about 'what God will do' in such definitive terms that if those things don't happen in the way the leader promised they would, people are disappointed and deeply disillusioned.

The controlling leader

Out of insecurity and poor training, there are leaders who cannot share power. They feel threatened if they are not in control, and in one way or another they ensure that every road leads to them. They make all the major decisions, and they have real difficulty in letting go.

Sometimes, particularly in pioneering situations, strong

leadership is what is needed and can be very positive. Pioneer leaders are good at working with young Christians – Christians of whatever age who are young in their faith. But with the leader's insecurities and inability to share leadership, there is a serious problem once those Christians become mature in their faith.

This weakness is rampant in established, denominational churches – but you can also see this in new churches. All around the country there are frustrated and disillusioned Christians who are desperate for a share of the action, but they can't get a look-in because of their leaders.

One of the things that theological colleges and training institutions need to consider is that leaders need as much training in the soft skills – how to listen to people, how to delegate, how to build teams – as the hard skills, such as knowing the Bible and leading meetings.

The abstract leader

Quite frankly, there are many Christian leaders who are just not leaders. Sometimes what is called 'the Peter principle' has happened, where they have been promoted beyond their level of competency. In other cases, because they have had a certain type of training, or perhaps were close to the previous leader, they are placed in a position of leadership that they are just not suited to. This happens in both denominational and new churches.

The thing that is most difficult about this particular category of leader is that they are often wonderful, pleasant people with godly character. But the truth remains that they do not have the spiritual skills, competency of character, or the calling of God to lead properly. This means that the churches they lead are frustrating places for those who want to grow spiritually, to make a difference in the world and to have a positive impact in their neighbourhood.

The character-weak leader

Christian leaders who are real hypocrites – highly selfish, or living in secret, active sin – are at one end of the scale. At the other end are leaders who simply have major character weaknesses. Again, I don't want to judge. Sometimes the leader who falls into sin should be treated with more sensitivity and kindness than we in the Church have sometimes given them.

The Church has a reputation for taking out its wounded and shooting them, rather than acknowledging the problem. Yes, perhaps remove these fallen leaders from leadership, but find ways of helping them change and be restored, instead of kicking them when they're down.

Nevertheless, these leaders do cause tremendous disillusionment. There are many Christians who have been mortified that the man or woman of God who they trusted, who they allowed to speak into their lives, was in fact behind the scenes an alcoholic, an embezzler, or involved in an immoral sexual relationship.

One of the saddest things in Christian circles today is hearing how people talk about some very well-known Christian leaders. They won't be mentioning the strengths or dynamism that the leaders have. Instead, they will be describing character weaknesses that in the early days of their ministry were masked by their strengths. It is inevitable that the longer people are around Christian leaders, the more they will see their weaknesses, and in the end a horrible price is paid by all.

One example of a character-weak leader might be someone who cannot confront people – that very nice leader who only wants to like people, and cannot deal with the problems and difficulties. This leader will not speak into other people's lives, and in the end will allow problem situations to escalate when they should have been dealt with a long time before.

The opinionated leader

This great person has all sorts of ideas, and the best ideas are always their ideas. Yes, their ideas might be good, and sometimes they are from God. And initially, these leaders are great to be around. But in the long term it can be disastrous because this leader feels that he or she is the only person with good and godly ideas.

In the meantime, church members grow increasingly frustrated because they want to be part of what is happening. These leaders don't listen, and in the end this creates feelings of low value and self-esteem in the lives of those around them.

The non-relational leader

There are also leaders who simply do not have the skills to be relational. In the old days, this was not such a problem. People in leadership were seen as having truth and special skills that the 'ordinary people' did not have. Also, the expectations of the church members were different. They did not expect to have a relationship with their leader. Leaders were those strangely anointed people who were out there, set apart. Again, this was true in both denominational and non-denominational structures.

The fact is, though, that the world has changed, and the expectations of church members have altered radically. Many of them have as much skill and knowledge as their leaders. Some have more. Education in general is at a much higher level.

People's understanding of church has changed. Yes, they want leadership, but they don't expect their leaders to be 'set apart' or special. They also expect to be involved in their church, and to have some form of relationship with their leaders.

With the non-relational leader, even though he or she might have some good qualities, there is often a slow spreading of disillusionment and difficulty.

Unfulfilled vision and destiny

The disillusioned Christian may have had a dream in their heart and a sense of calling from God. Yet as they look back on their lives, the dream, the calling, the ministry, hasn't happened. Perhaps fifteen or twenty years into their Christian life, they feel a victim of their circumstances, a spiritual failure, a non-entity.

Where was God? What happened? The clouds of disillusionment are thick and dark, and the dream is a faint memory. They might even give up being a practising Christian.

Of course, there could be all sorts of reasons why this situation has happened. The person might have been involved in a church or Christian organisation that had some of the leadership types mentioned above and may never have been given room for their gifts or calling. Perhaps they have suffered as a result of their own character weaknesses. Or they feel that life has simply been tough for them – they were never in the right place at the right time, and it was other people who got all the breaks.

They could have found themselves caught up in a difficult marriage, with children who took up vast amounts of time. Or they could have been in a demanding job that consumed every working and waking hour, never giving them the freedom and opportunity to pursue other things.

They feel that life has controlled them. They were swept up in a river that moved so fast they could never pause for breath, or take positive steps towards their dream. Maybe you can relate to this kind of disillusionment.

There are many reasons why dreams and visions are not fulfilled, whether through structures people have been involved in, lack of opportunities, or just the plain old difficulties of life.

Perhaps another reason is our own misunderstanding of the ways of God. Something common to many disillusioned people is a theology that implies that God will do everything. They have faithfully waited for God, but the sad thing is that maybe God has been waiting for them. Sometimes our poor theology has not stressed enough that we have to play our own part in God's purposes, and not just sit around waiting for him to act.

Relationships

A common cause of pain and disillusionment is friendships and relationships that have gone wrong. Christians rightly stress the relational nature of Christianity – the relationship between God and us, but also the relationships we have with each other as part of a loving community. The reality for many of us, though, is that as we enter into the joy of the Christian family, we sometimes experience relationships that go wrong.

Of course, this happens with relationships outside the Church as well, maybe with family members or work colleagues. Relationships are steeped in pain and brokenness, and this forms a particularly dark and disturbing cloud over many lives.

It is not the purpose of this book to look at why relationships turn sour. Each broken relationship carries its own tragic and painful story. Later, though, I want to pursue some principles that will set us free.

We might feel that a relationship has begun to feel tired and dull. If there is a relationship that has grown difficult, it wears us thin emotionally and spiritually and we feel pretty exposed.

Ourselves

Of course, we are quite capable of causing our own disillusionment. You might have failed yourself, by sinning, letting people down, or even letting yourself down. Sometimes this can be through your own rebellious choice. You have deliberately done the things that you ought not to have done, and you have paid a price.

In some cases, it might not be as simple as that. Perhaps at the time, you did not know any better. You thought you were doing okay. In my story in Chapter 1, my inability to confront people created huge problems for everyone. My own weakness, that I felt I could do very little about, created disillusionment for me.

Perhaps you are going through a mid-life crisis. Your children did not turn out as you hoped they might, your relationships and friendships have not prospered as you expected, and perhaps your marriage is a shadow of what it could have been.

There is also the fact that most of us will, at some time or another, arrive at a place in our work life where we have not achieved all that we hoped for and a certain mundaneness has taken over. Many people have to face the reality that they may spend ten or twenty years on work they'd rather not do, with people they find it extremely hard to be with. I will look at this situation in more depth in a later chapter.

It is perfectly understandable to me why many women can end up feeling very angry and with some pretty dark clouds – in a Christian environment, in their family, or in the workplace. There is no doubt that women often draw the short straw.

At work, they may not get the respect or promotion opportunities that they deserve, although this situation is slowly changing as a result of legislation and much campaigning that has taken place over the last few decades.

Things aren't much better in many families. Maybe a young woman has been caught in a situation where her potential, her possibilities, the dreams that live inside her, have little chance of ever happening. Sadly, this may not change if or when she marries.

One example is Jane, who had all the potential of being a well-known artist, but her father decided that art school was something his daughter should never do. Later she married a man who, if he ever saw her paint, would snap her paintbrushes and tear up her artwork. Her talents, her dream, could never take place. Jane was trapped in an environment that was far from positive, yet her faith sustained her.

Many women have sacrificially taken on the lead role in raising children, and for a lot of them this is a dream fulfilled. This is what they wanted to do. But for others, it is a mixed blessing.

If we look at the role of women in the Church and are brutally honest with ourselves, we have to put our hands up and admit, 'We have not done well.'

Things have improved somewhat. There are many fantastic women who have persevered through the most difficult circumstances, served, prayed and given of themselves. Without their vital contribution, the Church would not be what it is. Sadly, though, there are others who have been crushed. They have understandably ended up under dark clouds. The Church has not provided the environment for them to exploit the calling and destiny that God has for their lives.

Another difficult area is how we deal with our own children. Children can bring great joy to their parents. But the fact is that while many parents have done the best they could to bring up their children with the understanding and resources that they had, perhaps through no fault of their own they have ended up loving children who have caused great disillusionment and dark clouds of pain and disappointment.

This has to be one of the hardest challenges in life. The

finger of accusation will point at those parents, with the stinging words: 'It's your fault,' even though actually it may not have been.

There are many parents who are tortured with the thought: 'Perhaps we could have done things differently. Even though we've done our best to walk with God, it hasn't turned out all roses. The clouds are dark, and the sunny days are few and far between.'

In this chapter, I have explored just some of the things that cause disillusionment. Perhaps you can identify with some of them and definitely feel those clouds. All I can say is, read on.

As we go on to look at some of the answers, you may not be able to make the clouds totally disappear, but you can learn to live with them in such a way that they no longer have such power to shape your life.

As we look at the stories of others, the clouds might become companions that drift alongside you. They will be old enemies, but beyond them you will be able to see the sun once again.

The clouds do not cover the whole sky. The dream shines through, God is bigger than the problem, and you *can* regain your hope.

5

Steps to Freedom from Pain

As people attempt to cope with pain, many confusing thoughts race through their minds: *Who did this? Whose fault is it? God's? Mine? That person out there?*

Then there are very practical questions, like: *How do I get out of bed this morning? How can I face tomorrow? Is it worth facing tomorrow? How on earth can I do my job today?*

In the midst of a crisis, people's emotions, thoughts and feelings are all over the place. In no particular order then, here are a few suggestions for living with and handling our pain.

To start with, there's the God question

One of the saddest stories I know of involves a couple whose young child accidentally kicked a ball on to a road through the garden gates. As is the way of little children, he shot after it with no thought to danger or safety, just 'Where is my ball?' Tragically, a young driver, travelling much too fast, smashed into and killed him.

A number of years later, I talked with these very desperate parents. They had lost their Christian faith and were locked up in a prison of pain and darkness. They had been taught that bad things don't happen to Christians – if you have faith, these things just don't take place. When something tragic *did* take place, all they could believe was that they were victims of God's arbitrary sense of humour. They could no longer find it in their hearts to love or serve him in any way whatsoever. Given what they were taught, their response was understandable.

But this teaching is nowhere in the Bible. If you look closely at scripture, what you don't see is that the believer gets a better ride through life, that bad things don't happen to them, that they are protected from the selfishness of our society, or shielded from the diseases and the problems that are in the world.

What you *do* see is that the non-believer faces these pains and difficulties more or less on their own – at best they have friends and family to help them. Believers, on the other hand, do not live in a closed system. They face these difficulties with the fantastic promise of Emmanuel God: 'Never will I leave you. Never will I forsake you' (Hebrews 13:5).

What we have in Christianity is the promise of relationship with God through Christ. We have the possibility of intimacy and communication. We also have the promise of eternal life, that we will be with him for ever. There is no promise for the absence of difficulty or pain, but there *is* the promise of help in time of need.

Sometimes we don't claim this promise initially. Our early reaction to pain and difficulty is that it must be somebody's fault, and our raw emotions and pain will tell us (wrongly) that God is far away.

Psalm 10 is a good example of this. It begins with the question: 'Why, O Lord, do you stand far off? Why do you hide yourself in times of trouble?' (v. 1).

The first eleven verses in this psalm show the pouring out of a heart experiencing intense pain. We might read them as quiet words on a page, but they were most likely uttered with tears, shouts and great moans.

God is used to being shouted at. It's all part of the deal of relationship. He doesn't mind. Shout, cry and scream. God knows your heart, so be honest with where you are emotionally.

There is a natural progression in the psalm. By the time we get to verse 14, the psalmist is finally putting his feet on solid ground. He is declaring that God *does* see, that he *will* take notice. He is ending the psalm as positively as he can in the light of the difficult circumstances.

The first secret of dealing with pain is: talk to God

Shout if you must, but tell him what you are going through, not just once but every day.

How will God answer this cry? Verse 17 of the psalm tells us two things: that God will listen, and that he will give us courage. Courage is another word for strength and endurance. You might just need the strength to get out of bed and face the world.

God listening and giving us courage are, I believe, universal promises for us all. What is not so universal is how God steps in. In some cases, we will hear miraculous stories of healing, maybe even instantaneous healing. In other cases, as in my own story at the start of this book, the answer took three to four years in coming. Sometimes there *isn't* an answer in terms of the pain disappearing. A loved one has died, or is dying, and God might answer by giving us the courage to endure and find peace. We need to come to the realisation that God cannot remove all the difficulties and pain from the world. It is only in heaven that we will eventually find a pain-free environment.

Taking ownership

If the first step is talking to God and the second is being honest, the third step is ownership. A very common reaction to difficulty is to deny its existence – to pretend it's not there. It seems extraordinary, looking from the outside, that people often want to pretend that their pain is not there, i.e. they are not ill or the relationship hasn't broken down. But the sooner we face the reality of saying it *is* there, the sooner we will be able to talk to God about it. That might be hard if our feelings tell us he doesn't care, but we need to take a step of faith.

Abiding in and practising the presence of Christ

We also need to abide in Christ. In John 15 there is the story of the vine, which is all about abiding in and focusing on Christ.

> I am the vine, you are the branches. He who abides in me, and I in him, he it is that bears much fruit.
>
> (John 15:5)

Admitting that we have pain and then looking to Christ is perhaps, as C. S. Lewis argued, what pain is all about. Pain is the body's natural mechanism to tell us we need help.

There are many places people go to for help. Some are destructive, be they alcohol abuse, drugs, denial, or even walking away from God, which might be our natural reaction. Perhaps the hardest step of faith for people in pain is to say, 'God, you are there. You are listening, and I will focus on you,' while everything inside them is screaming: 'You're kidding. God is on holiday. God doesn't care.' Focusing on Christ, abiding in the presence of Jesus, takes honest prayer.

God, by definition of being God, knows all about our pain and difficulty. But God steps into our situation when we acknowledge our pain and abide in Christ – when we are honest in prayer.

Again, as you meditate on Psalm 10, you see the anger and pain of the psalmist. This is the process of abiding, when in essence he is saying: 'Dear God, I am in real pain down here. Where are you? Don't you see? Don't you care?' Then he comes to that faith moment: 'Even though I can't see you or feel you, you are who you say you are.'

By our articulation, by our prayer, we give God permission to step in.

If we focus on the presence of God in times of pain, God will give us courage (see Psalm 10:17). There is also the promise that God will not let us be tested beyond what we can endure (1 Corinthians 10:13), and that God's grace will be sufficient for us.

This brings us to a difficult theological issue. When it comes to pain, the grace of God manifests itself in two ways:

First, it manifests itself by giving day-by-day strength to people in pain. For example, Michael, whose wife has the severest and most crippling form of multiple sclerosis, has seen no healing or remission in her illness. But their courage, despite a downward day-by-day deterioration, testifies to the fact that God gives grace, strength and courage to endure.

Second, one also hears stories of the presence of God intervening to take the pain away, be it supernatural healing or perhaps a medical breakthrough. Ailish and I, as we spent two years focusing on the presence of God in the midst of our pain, saw a medical answer for Justyn, as well as changes in ourselves that brought breakthrough.

The fact that God shows his presence in two very distinct ways is a huge problem to the body of Christ, and we need to be honest about this problem. For some, the presence of God will bring healing. For others, it will give grace to endure.

Instead of always saying that God will bring healing and the pain will go away, we need to encourage people to focus on Christ, abide in his presence and leave it up to God which of the two ways he manifests his presence. If we really trust in the love of God, that trust should not be dependent on how he decides to manifest his presence in our lives.

Following on from this, the natural question is: should we actively pursue healing, or just accept the pain and difficulty? I'll be honest: this is a difficult question to answer. Ailish and I cried for a breakthrough, praying without ceasing. Yes, we needed to be open to the healing/break-through option, but not to the extent that it was the only option.

It is an amazing testimony that the body of Christ, throughout church history, has faced pain and difficulty with incredible dignity, grace and joy. Even in the midst of our pain, the presence of Jesus is still with us.

Recently I went to the funeral of an eight-year-old boy who had tragically died of cancer. Yet there was a powerful testimony of the presence of God helping his mother and father in the midst of their suffering.

I have spoken of practising the presence of God through being honest, then focusing on Jesus. But there are many other ways that Christians have traditionally cultivated the presence of God, be it by the breaking of bread in communion, by reflective or quiet prayer, by standing in front of a picturesque landscape and contemplating the beauty of God – the list is endless.

For some it might be standing on a beach in the midst of a storm, for others walking and praying. Whatever way works best for you, it is all about focusing on the presence of Jesus.

Connecting with the body of Christ

Honesty has two aspects to it: being honest with God, but also being honest with your fellow Christians. When we are experiencing times of great difficulty, there is a tremendous temptation to keep it to ourselves. We don't want to be a bother, we don't want to dump on people, and we hold back. There is also the fear of what others might think. *Will I be rejected? Will I go down in their estimation?*

These are common apprehensions, but I actually believe that your connection with the body of Christ will be a major resource through which the Holy Spirit can bring strength and encouragement to help you through. Praying in times of pain is vital, but it is hard to experience a sense of God in those prayers. It is also hard to read the scriptures, and during a time of pain, reading your Bible may just be a daily discipline with nothing much sinking in. Others may not want to read the Bible at all.

So being connected to the body of Christ in some way is essential. Generally, those who stay connected to the body, to Christian friends and leadership, are the ones who make it. The ones who tough it out on their own, for whatever reason, are often the ones who don't make it.

This is not to limit God and say that God can't help you in isolation. But surely you need to keep open as many avenues as possible for God to step in and strengthen you, and God might want to do this through your brothers and sisters in Christ.

Ailish and I certainly found 'being connected' very important. When the difficulties first arose, well-meaning people advised me: 'Laurence, you must keep this quiet. You are the director of a large youth ministry. It is not good for people to know that you are going through a major crisis.'

This struck me as ridiculous, and we made a very conscious and deliberate choice to connect with the body in three ways. First, there was what I call 'the friend connection'. Ailish and I had cultivated a number of friendships over the years, and by means of a newsletter we kept twelve of the closest in touch on a monthly basis, being honest and asking for prayer. As well as this, we contacted our closest four or five friends by phone and discussed the situation with them.

When difficulties are ongoing, personal friendships are vital, and are sometimes the source of breakthrough moments.

I will never forget when Justyn ran off one Christmas Day, after having been particularly difficult. Ailish was crying in one room, the girls were crying in another, and I was sitting at the dining-room table in what felt like deep, terminal despair. In the midst of this, the phone rang. It was my friend, Michael, and his words went something like:

'Laurence, I know you're going through a hard time right now, and this is a bleak day, but I just wanted to tell you that I'm your friend. I am committed to you, and I know that somehow and in some way you are going to get through this.'

Up until this time, it had been very hard to sense God in any way in the difficulties. Yet suddenly, through this phone call, it was as if God himself was saying to me: 'It is all right. I am here with you. You are not on your own.'

For the first time in months, a glimmer of hope lit up in my heart. *There is a pathway out of this situation. There is a possibility of overcoming.*

As well as personal friendships, there was our connection to our local church. In our case, this was at a cell or small group level, and we also had contact with our overall pastor. We informed people of what was going on in our lives, and we asked for their support and help.

Our third way of 'connecting' during the difficulties was seeking professional help. In the case of physical illness, this will have been your first step. But in relational breakdowns involving husbands, wives or children, this either isn't done, or comes only as a last resort. Professionals will tell you that they are often called in too late, and/or when they *are* called in at least one of the parties involved is not open for serious help.

If you ask for help, be it professional or from Christian friends, you must be prepared to receive it. You should also be able to take advice.

I don't know about you, but I'm not always good at taking advice. I have not been open to people telling me what I have done right or wrong. If you are dealing with physical pain, you may have done nothing wrong whatsoever. But if you are dealing with relational pain, such as broken relationships, it might be that you are partly responsible for the problem, and therefore have some responsibility for the solution.

Receiving help

Pain often makes us more open to receiving help and advice. This openness will almost certainly be essential in getting through the difficulty.

A psychologist I was seeing told me: 'Laurence, I can give you advice, but do you want it, and will you do anything about it? If not, all we are doing is playing games.'

In the midst of your pain and difficulty, this kind of tough attitude might seem offensive. Your desire for a sticking plaster and an instant solution is understandable. But this bridge must be crossed. In seeking professional help, you must *really* want help, and also be prepared to change.

As I explained earlier, a major factor in our personal difficulties was what my psychologist called the Harrods syndrome: my inability to confront people; my own internal deception that took away any feelings of anger; and my fear of laying down boundaries. Even though we received some medical help, which included prescription drugs for Justyn, it was only half the answer. The other half involved a dramatic and extremely painful change in the way that we parented.

Ailish and I had what we thought was a healthy balance. She was tough and had boundaries. I was accepting and had no boundaries. This, we felt, was perfect parenting, and with our first child, Kiera, it had seemed to work quite well. But we had to face the fact that what was good for one child was not necessarily good for another. Change was required.

The professional psychologist gave me tough advice when he said: 'Laurence, you will always feel that Ailish is too strong and too hard. Because of the Harrods syndrome, you will always want to downplay her answers. You will feel inside yourself a tremendous sense that your soft approach is right and her tough approach is wrong. But you need to listen. Your emotional response is not right and cannot be trusted. It is dysfunctional.'

In theory, this sounds fine. But the next time a situation arose and Ailish drew a line, everything inside me wanted to undo that line. Everything inside me said she was wrong. It was extremely difficult to fight my feelings and listen to the dim voice of the psychologist. All sorts of self-justifying thoughts sprang to mind. *Don't I make good decisions?* I felt as if I was betraying myself.

The Harrods syndrome was my dysfunction. You might have a problem with the way you listen to people, or treat them. You might get cross or aggressive very easily. If you have a dysfunction, whatever it is will have to be faced and dealt with.

The psychologist pushed me on to the next step when he said: 'Laurence, you have to stand up to Justyn and shout. He cannot read body language very well. He needs to see clearly that you are not happy. His behaviour is unacceptable, and you need to love him enough to tell him so. This is not the right time to take him to Harrods, saying, "There, there, it's all right." '

This was difficult for me, for two reasons. One, I have never shouted at anyone in my life. Two, just listening to shouting makes me feel ill. The memories of my own childhood, with the shouting I had seen and witnessed, made the thought of me raising my own voice deliberately almost impossible. When pushed, like everyone, I could get angry. But that would always be at the end of a situation. What I had to learn was to lay down boundaries, not out of anger and frustration, not out of losing control, but at the beginning of a situation when I was still in control.

Some of you might think: 'So, what's the problem?' Bear in mind that what is easy for some might be extremely difficult for others, and what is easy for others might be unimaginably difficult for you. In a sense, we all have something difficult in our lives that needs to be faced.

Building new habits

Ailish and I had to come to that place where we were in harmony and agreement on the daily incidents we were facing. Me stepping into those instances, rather than her, involved a learning process that took about a year and a half. Old habits do not disappear overnight. Building new ones takes time.

Do you not know that if you yield yourselves to any one as obedient slaves, you are slaves of the one whom you obey, either of sin, which leads to death, or of obedience, which leads to righteousness?

(Romans 6:16)

In this verse from Romans, we see that we become slaves to the one whom we obey. This includes being slaves to our old habits.

With every habit, two processes take place. If we do something on a repeated basis, it becomes a habit, and we soon get locked into that habit, just like a padlock. If the habit is sinful and against the principles of God's truth, the padlock has a sin dynamic to it.

The pathway to freedom from this bad habit has two aspects. The first involves confession and repentance. The second involves trusting in the grace of God to build a new habit pattern so that we become slaves of righteousness. Paradoxically, when we become 'slaves' of righteousness we are truly free.

The other side to this is that there are many habit patterns we might step into which in a sense are not sinful. I call these character weaknesses. They are learned responses, and although not strictly sinful, they are still not helpful, and we are still padlocked into them. Freedom from these habit patterns is a little bit different from those with a sin dynamic.

The one I illustrated in my own story – not being able to confront – was a deep-seated habit which affected my emotions and every part of my personality. Psychiatrists and other professional helpers are good at identifying unhelpful patterns, pointing out the problem, but they are not always able to give solutions.

Christians have an advantage in that they can go to God and ask for help. God can break the power of that padlock, but then comes the hard bit: day-by-day choosing to live differently.

In my case, this involved stepping into situations rather than shying away from them. This was hard. For years, my inner mechanism told me that my bad habit pattern was in fact good. This mechanism still tried to encourage me to live as I had always lived. This felt peculiar, almost wrong, even though it was in fact right.

The good news – and many experts have confirmed this – is that if we perform any action between thirty-two and sixty-four times, we create a new habit pattern. We reinforce it in our lives. So every time I laid down boundaries in the family it became easier. The strange feelings slowly faded.

In rebuilding your habit patterns, whatever they may be, you might need strong encouragement and help, particularly if the habit pattern is of a longstanding nature. You and God on your own may not be enough. You might need to meet with God in the Christian body, as it were, with people praying regularly for you and standing with you in support.

I once knew a man called Paul who had a habit pattern of self-mutilation. His arms were covered in scars. He had been cutting himself for many, many years, and it was a way of life for him. But the process out of this habit pattern started when Paul asked for help. Christian counsellors were able to show him some of the roots of his problem, such as old hurts and insecurities. Those supporting Paul cried out to God, believing that he would break the padlock, as it were. They also prayed that God would give Paul day-by-day strength to live a new way.

In this case, they also knew it would be most helpful if, when he had the urge to cut himself, Paul could go and pray with an individual. So a number of Christians made themselves available. Over a period of two years, Paul created, slowly but surely, a brand new habit pattern. It took time, it was a process, but in the end he was completely set free from the habit of self-mutilation.

As you can see, there are times when freedom from pain is dependent on us changing as well. We have developed habit patterns, ways of life, that are part of the problem. It feels most unfair to us that we have all this pain, yet we also have to deal with our own problems. This is part of the pathway to freedom.

However, there may be many other occasions when we are experiencing pain – maybe as the result of a bereavement or an ongoing sickness – and there isn't a character weakness or problem in our lives that is contributing to it.

In these situations, there are three areas that we need to come to terms with. The first area covers all of the emotions and feelings inside us that the pain is causing.

The second involves our underlying doubts, if we have them: 'How can a God who is meant to love allow this to happen to me?'

Third, we can feel extremely bad about ourselves. We somehow feel guilty, even though we have done nothing at all to cause the pain. This guilt has a negative impact on how we see ourselves, and it causes us to feel isolated from God. Our inclination is to withdraw from the body of Christ, but if we do this, our pain and isolation is compounded and the pathways to freedom are limited.

As we've already seen, instead of withdrawing, the process of coping should start with honesty: *It hurts down here. Life is not fair.*

One major area of pain that all of us have to face at some point is grief. Whether it is through the death of a loved one, a child, a close friend, a parent or partner, it will be an intense and difficult time, with the intensity varying, depending on whether we feel robbed. Has that person died unexpectedly? Is it a child or a partner who is still very young? A parent who is not very old?

It might be helpful at this point if I tell three stories. The first concerns a young man whom we will call Chris. Chris was twenty-one and had only been a Christian for a few months when he found himself caring for his dying father, who was just fifty-four.

There was one benefit to Chris being a young Christian – his faith was still unsophisticated; he wasn't disillusioned. But it was also untried and untested.

Chris had become a Christian in a foreign land and knew no Christians in his home country, so on his return home he would be on his own. When he was about to catch a plane to come back to this country to care for his sick father, a more mature Christian had advised him, 'Whatever happens, whatever you experience, whether you feel it or not, Jesus will be with you.'

This simple piece of theology was all that Chris knew. As he began to look after his sick father, wash him, clean up the vomit, deal with the painful nitty-gritty of caring – something he had never done for anyone in his entire life –

he repeated to himself on a daily basis what this Christian had said to him. He talked to God about his loneliness and how revolted he was by what he had to do. Then he re-minded God of the promise that Jesus would be with him, and he asked him to help him survive the day.

The day came when he and his brothers stood by the hospital bed with their dying father. Through the pain and hard times, a strong relationship had developed between Chris and his father. God was making good through the difficulty. Then his father's breathing stopped and he had gone.

The most appalling sense of loneliness and isolation filled the room. Chris looked at his two brothers and saw their loneliness and pain, and he felt just as alone as they were. He didn't really know if his father was a Christian or not. All he knew was that he had gone, that he would not be there tomorrow, and he felt deep sorrow for all those won-derful moments that would now never be.

Chris also knew, though, that there was a spiritual dimen-sion for him that wasn't there for his brothers. Silently, he prayed a quick prayer: 'God, it doesn't feel as if you're really here. I can't see you. I can't feel you. This is bad. Are you here?'

It didn't take long for Chris to add to his prayer: 'Yes, I know you are here.'

When Chris's prayer was answered, everything was differ-ent. Chris no longer felt alone. He knew somehow that God's love for his father was as intense and passionate as his own. He sensed God's grieving, and was comforted by this. He also knew that this was a comfort his own brothers would not experience.

Another tragedy we may face one day is the death of a partner. The grief is obviously more intense when it happens unexpectedly and the partner is relatively young. When this happens, psychologists tell us that the flight and fight syndrome will often kick in, with the body producing large quantities of adrenaline to counteract the effects of the tragedy. Occasionally, this causes an almost false sense of cheerfulness. Sometimes, people who are in the midst of a most awful bereavement appear to be quite cheerful in the early stages, and there seems to be a slight unreality to the whole situation. Slowly but surely, the grief, the pain and the reality sink in.

Kristy was twenty-nine, a mother with two little girls. The youngest was only a few months old when Kristy's husband, Gary, was diagnosed with cancer. To start with, the cancer did not appear to be too serious. Unfortunately, one of the operations didn't work, and after a few months he died. Kristy, who was a missionary in a foreign country, was left totally penniless. Gary had no pension, no savings, no insurance of any description, and Kristy still had these two little girls to look after.

At the beginning she felt fine, and many people were supporting her. But slowly and surely, the reality of her situation came upon her. Day by day she had to face the difficulty of bringing up these two little girls on her own, with no resources.

Everything inside her told her that God had been random and arbitrary in this situation. Why her? Why not someone else? She even felt that God had abandoned her, and that she and her girls would suffer years of difficulty.

Kristy told me later that after these disturbing thoughts

and emotions had raged in her mind and heart, she had to make a conscious choice: 'Either God was who he said he was, the God of the scriptures, and I needed to believe that. Or I could do a deal with him, saying, "If you tell me why this happened to me, I'll believe in you again." I could have even just walked away from my faith.'

Kristy knew that the real challenge was to believe God to be true to who he was in the scriptures, while her questions remained unanswered. She told me that one dark and tearful night, when she felt particularly alone in her small room, 'I made a declaration. Not only was God exactly who he said he was, he would also be a father for these two girls. In some way, he would provide the comfort, the strength and the provision we needed as a family.'

Some fifteen years after this experience, Kristy told me a fantastic story of how, through what seemed to be miraculous intervention that involved the body of Christ, she had been awarded a British widow's pension. At first she had been told that she wasn't eligible for this, but in the end it came through. The mission agency her husband had worked for provided accommodation at a minimal rent. Also, in extraordinary ways, her children had been provided for.

At this point, Kristy has not re-married, but she has found comfort and friendship in her relationship with God. She made the right choice – God has been faithful to her and her family.

Every time Christians act sacrificially and lovingly to one another, it is not just a human act but carries something of the presence of God.

The family I mentioned before, who lost their eight-year-old boy through cancer, described something wonderful that happened in the last two weeks of his life. Every morning when this family opened their front door, their doormat had become a bed of primroses. Each night, someone was spending a considerable amount of time threading primroses into the doormat.

For their twelve-year-old daughter, who knew that she was in the process of losing her brother, this was a wondrous thing. Every morning she would see this token of love and care. Its impact was not just the normal impact you would expect from a kind human endeavour – for the Christians receiving it, it was an indication of God's love and care. It gave them hope and strength.

Learning through experience

Another way of dealing with pain is to recognise that its impact is not all bad. People going through a pain experience may well end up as better people.

The Apostle Paul has an interesting little phrase: 'death is at work in us, but life in you' (2 Corinthians 4:12). Here he is hinting at two things. First, in an earlier analogy Paul talks about treasure in earthen vessels, even though earthen vessels can be imperfect or broken in some way. Often, people's faith is stronger, and their life is richer and more enhanced, because they have survived through their difficulties. The treasure inside the vessel shines through in a greater way.

Second, Paul implies that the 'death' experience – or time of difficulty – we might have been through, brings life to others in a very real way.

There is no doubt that if we read through scripture –

whether we look at the story of Job, the life of Moses, the themes in Psalm 23, or Jesus himself – we will see that God uses the trials and tribulations that we go through, the pain and the difficulty, to refine us, and in the end make us better people.

This is not to say that God is the author of those difficulties, but it *is* to say that he will work in those difficulties. There can be a positive outcome to your pain.

From my own personal experience, I can honestly look back and say that I hated every moment of what I went through. Hopefully, though, I am a better person because of those experiences.

Life has come from 'death'.

6

Overcoming Disillusionment

In previous chapters I've used the analogy of a cloud to represent the disillusionment that blocks your vision and dominates everything you see. The bright sun that you once knew lived beyond the clouds now seems far away. So, how can you make the cloud move?

The first important thing to realise is that you will never totally remove the cloud. Humans have memories. We have emotions and feelings and set patterns of behaviour. God does not wave a magic wand that removes all these things as if they were never there. The important thing is to move them to one side so that you can see the sun – to live in the power of your dreams and expectations, rather than being shaped by the cloud. But even just moving them is not an easy task.

While we explore the various elements that will make this possible, it is good to bear in mind that there is no set formula. I will be laying out in this chapter a number of thoughts, ideas and biblical principles that are important. You will need to decide, in co-operation with the Holy Spirit, which ones are best for you.

One of the most remarkable figures in the New Testament is the Apostle Paul. He was betrayed and let down by his friends on many occasions. He was disappointed by senior Christian leaders, such as Peter, who did not always behave as he thought they should. He suffered the breakdown of his close relationship with Barnabas. He was beaten and left for dead, shipwrecked, locked up in prison and left to rot and die. This is appalling stuff, yet his letters contain some of the most moving sentences ever written. In spite of all his suffering, his faith still shines through. As he writes in Philippians 3:14: 'I press on toward the goal for the prize of the upward call of God in Christ Jesus.'

What was his secret? What enabled Paul to live this way? You might want to answer: 'He was special. He was an Apostle. He was made of different stuff than us.' But the truth is that he was just like us. What helped him was that he had discovered some important Christian principles.

One of the principles is right at the start of the book of Romans, where Paul says he is 'a servant of Jesus Christ' (Romans 1:1). The word 'servant' that he uses can literally be translated as 'slave'. Paul is calling himself 'a slave of Jesus Christ', because he had recognised right from the beginning of his Christian life that as far as Christ was concerned he had no rights.

Paul came from a background where rights were important. As a senior Judaic figure, as a student of the law and as a Roman citizen, he was well aware of his position in society and the rights he had as a free person. Yet he realised that surrender to the love of Christ and having Jesus at the centre of his life meant that he laid his rights down. As a result, he knew the presence of Jesus.

Giving up rights

In writing this chapter, I could look at some of the easier ways of handling disillusionment and leave this one out. But this was the key to the Apostle Paul's life. If you have no rights – if everything in life is a privilege and you have exchanged your rights for the presence of God – then in one sense, your disillusionment and disappointments will have no power over you.

If you live by this principle, you don't have expectations that church must always go well for you, that leaders must do what is right, that relationships must always work out well, or whatever rights you feel you might have.

The fact is that we live in a fallen world, and many of the causes of disillusionment are simply the fruit of the world we live in. As soon as we get this sense of not having any rights in our Christian life, disillusionment no longer needs to be in front of us. The clouds will slip to one side.

Understanding who God is

We also see from Paul that he doesn't blame God. His picture of God, despite all the hard times, remains vital and alive. Perhaps the most important thing you need to maintain in your Christian life is a dynamic understanding of who God is. In other words, you need some good theology.

If your view of God is flawed – if you see God as the author and the shaper of your difficulties, or even as the one who passively allows them to happen – it is going to be difficult to walk free from your disillusionment.

Jesus, when he taught us to pray, gave us a model called the Lord's Prayer:

> Our Father who art in heaven,
> Hallowed be thy name.
> Thy Kingdom come,
> Thy will be done,
> On earth as it is in heaven.
> Give us this day our daily bread;
> And forgive us our debts,
> As we also have forgiven our debtors;
> And lead us not into temptation,
> But deliver us from evil.

(Matthew 6:9–13)

It is interesting to see how this prayer is laid out. It begins by making you think about God – who and where God is. This is before you worship or do anything else.

Before you get to that step, though, you need to think of something else. In dealing with your pain in prayer, you need to begin with it. As we saw in Psalm 10, you need to be honest with God and describe your pain – what has happened, and how it has affected you. Ailish and I, in dealing with our son, talked with God every morning about the pain of the day before. We needed to process it – describe it.

Describing your pain

The same is true with your disillusionment. Begin your prayer with description: what happened; what you experienced; what you felt. It doesn't matter whether your feelings are justified, whether you are right or wrong to feel them. The fact is that you do, and you need to describe them.

My personal recommendation is that your description of your pain and disillusionment is something that is done out loud between you and God. In the psalms, David described his struggles in all their nitty-gritty, gruesome details.

Yes, God already knows – Christians believe that God knows everything there is to know, because God is by definition God. But just knowing that God knows is very non-relational. It is not personal, not cathartic, and it doesn't particularly help you. But when you speak out what you are experiencing, it becomes personal, and in a sense you are giving God permission to be involved.

The descriptive process is not always easy, sometimes because in your disillusionment you are angry with God as well. Don't worry about this. Whatever you say to God, he will remain solid throughout. My own personal experience is that I have never shocked God. God knows I think these things, that I am suffering these torments and pains. However dark your thoughts are, and whether they represent reality or just how you feel, I believe that God is pleased with you sharing them.

But you cannot stop there. Just like the beginning of the Lord's Prayer, you need to look at how you see God. Is the God you serve shaped by your feelings, by the descriptions or accusations that you have poured out to God? Or is God different from them? Of course God is, even though you can't fully sense that through the cloud of disillusionment.

This is the hardest part: to believe what you cannot see;

to trust in what you do not feel; to love that which, at this point, your emotions tell you to hate; to give your future to someone you think is doing a really bad job right now. This is an extremely difficult process. It can only really be done by taking a slight step backwards and remembering God's nature: 'Our Father, who art in heaven'.

This reference to parenthood describes to us the innate nature of God: God is our father and mother.

It is important to say here that God is not solely masculine (Deuteronomy 32:18; Galatians 3:28). We are made in God's image, and we are male and female (Genesis 1:27). We need to remember this. One of the great injustices of our time is the way many women have been treated by the body of Christ, and they are justifiably disillusioned.

Remember who you are going to when you pray: the ultimate source of love, the God who loved the world so much that the Father gave his only Son to be sacrificed for it (John 3:16). The biblical picture is that at the heart of the universe, whether you recognise this or not, there is a God who, in nature and very being, is sacrificial love.

The fact that God is in heaven can imply two things. One is God's power and authority – that ultimately, even if not in this world, there will be justice. God does have the power to step in (Jeremiah 32:17). Into even the darkest disillusionment, God's light can shine.

Second, it implies beauty. Heaven is a place of beauty and wonder. You will not always sense it or experience it, but nevertheless it is there. The beauty of heaven is infinitely greater than the reality you know.

Trust

So, after your description, expressing your thoughts and feelings to God, there has to be trust: 'God, you are who you say you are, even though I can only see the dark cloud right now. Beyond that cloud, there is love and beauty. My disillusionment does not shape you.'

The third step in prayer is one I have already mentioned: realising that you don't have any rights. You were not promised a disillusion-free journey.

You own nothing and expect nothing, except for the promised presence of Jesus. Yes, you have been let down or betrayed. So was Jesus. So was Paul.

In prayer, you must first describe, then you must trust, and then you have to hand over the right to feel the pain, the right to be angry. While you live in this fallen earth, while you are part of this frail human community, all your disillusionment is part of the everyday happenstance of life.

You must, by the grace of God, live beyond disillusionment. Don't ignore it. Don't bury it. Don't pretend it doesn't hurt. Instead, describe it. Give it over to a God you are trying to trust. Seek to move your disillusionment from in front of you to beside you.

When you realise that you have no right to be treated any differently from anyone else in this world, you really have surrendered all. Once you have done this, you can step actively into the presence of God. (There will be more about this in Chapter 7.)

Realistic expectations

In dealing with disillusionment, another principle to remember is realistic expectations.

In Chapter 4 I listed five areas disillusionment can come from in the Christian life. In order to get the maximum benefit and give the maximum contribution in each of these areas, you need to have realistic expectations. Unrealistic expectations will only lead to disappointment and disillusionment.

Church

Whether you're in a church of 'under-promise' or 'over-promise', or a church where leadership is not as helpful as it could be, you can still grow. The flaws in the church do not have to destroy your faith. What expectations do you have? You maybe need to ask yourself, 'Why church in the first place?'

Here's why. You can sum up the message of Jesus with three simple commands.

You are to love God

Before you can love God more fully, you need to know that you are loved by him. The fundamental revelation of the New Testament is that Christ died for all: 'For God so loved the world that he gave his only Son' (John 3:16). This simple sentence changes the value of every human being.

We are more than just a bunch of chemicals – we have eternal value. 'Christ died for all' includes you. No matter what your background is, or your personal circumstances, you are not the victim of these things, not what they say you are. *You are loved by God.*

In return, you are called to love and follow him, and to obey his commandments.

You are to love one another

Being a Christian is never something that can be done individually, as tempting as that might be. Community is at the heart of the Godhead: Father, Son and Holy Spirit. In other words, a Christian picture of a triune God is a picture of relationship: God the Father, Son and Holy Spirit in a dynamic relationship one to another, three persons in one. In this sense, we see community at the heart of the Godhead.

Jesus, in his time on earth, modelled community at various levels. The three members of the Trinity, the twelve disciples, the seventy, the 120, the multitudes.

He also spoke about it: 'By this all men will know that you are my disciples, if you have love for one another' (John 13:35).

Society today needs to see an expression of genuine community. People are disillusioned by the institutional side of church, but they are attracted when they see people of faith genuinely giving of their lives to each other.

You are to love the lost

You can do this in the context of your workplace, your neighbourhoods and churches, through being salt and light, and through personal relationships.

These three commands are our responsibilities as individuals, and church is the structure they are worked out in.

Sometimes church will help you do these things fantastically. You will have leaders and gifted individuals who, through their example, through leading small groups, through preaching and teaching, will inspire you to love God more. Brilliant.

Other times, though, you may go through phases when none of the above is taking place. In those circumstances, you are still called to be faithful. You must say to yourself: 'Whether I am helped or hindered by being part of the Church, this isn't the issue. What *is* the issue is I need to love God – and God has designed it so that his Church is one of the places I need to belong to as part of my love for him.'

You have to be part of a Christian community. Yes, there will be times when this is unbelievably difficult – when you are in small groups, cells or part of a congregation which has some very difficult people to love and care for. You, in turn, might be difficult for others to love and care for! But this does not take away from our responsibility to fulfil Jesus' commands.

Tony Campolo told a story of a friend of his who was a senior Christian leader. When his wife was seriously ill, this leader handed in his resignation. His friends challenged him and said that if he really loved God, surely he should stay in the ministry. His response was that he had made promises to his wife many years before, and he intended to keep them. He needed to look after her. Tony Campolo observed that his friend might not be happy with the situation, but he was a good man. He had chosen goodness over personal happiness.

In our modern society, hedonism, the pursuit of pleasure and the avoidance of pain, is a way of life. But we as

Christians are called to live differently. Our true love for God, for one another and for the lost, means that there will be many times when we must choose goodness over personal happiness.

As for loving the lost, I have to be honest and say that the Church as a whole hasn't had a very broad picture of what this means. A huge number of churches haven't been interested in what their congregations do from Monday to Friday, 7 a.m. to 7 p.m.

Happily, this has changed somewhat in recent years. Local churches and many Christian organisations have discovered a new emphasis and a fresh empowerment for this aspect of people's lives – helping people to bring God into the everyday, into the marketplace as it were.

You are as much a missionary if you take a sense of calling into your Monday-to-Friday existence as someone who works for and has been trained with a bona fide mission agency. You must take a personal responsibility to be salt and light in the world. If you're in a church that does not encourage you in this area, find some like-minded people out there who *can* support you.

Research has shown that friendship with non-Christians is the most effective form of evangelism. You can do this. Whether one friendship, three friendships, or more, you can find ways of reaching others in your workplace, your street, or your social and leisure activities.

If our realistic expectation is to influence a few and hopefully win a few in the course of our lifetime, we won't go far wrong. If church goes well, we will win and influence more. If, for whatever reason, church goes badly, we might win and influence fewer.

Once you have realistic expectations, you are protecting yourself from some of the ups and downs of being a Christian.

Christian leadership

In Chapter 4, I introduced certain types of Christian leaders who are bound to cause disappointment. During the course of your Christian life, you will inevitably meet some of these characters. As they say, to be forewarned is to be forearmed.

By the same token, I could just as easily have written a list of more positive Christian leaders, such as the caring leader, the praying leader or the wise teacher. Hopefully, you will have met some of these wonderful leaders whom God has raised up to equip and inspire his people. Other leaders might be a mixture of positive and negative. Some aspects of their ministry will be fantastically inspiring. Others will be a hindrance.

A realistic expectation in this case is to take all of the good things that come from Christian leaders, even if they are leaders with positive and negative aspects. On a personal note, I freely admit that my own leadership style has undoubtedly been mixed. I can look back at twenty-five years of ministry and see that I have encouraged a lot of people. But have I hurt and disillusioned other people, and disappointed them in the process? Unfortunately, the answer must be yes.

The only solution to this is that maturity is required early on in your Christian life. When the negative aspects of Christian leadership are affecting you, hold your own counsel and keep going, doing what you know is right.

When you meet a difficult leader, whether it is a controlling leader, abstract leader, character-weak leader, opinionated or non-relational leader, you have to be true to your convictions. Yes, these folks will affect you, but it will help you if you accept that they are human and support them as much as you can and allow forgiveness to flow. The most important thing is to have placed boundaries in your own soul of what you feel being obedient to Christ looks like, and press on regardless.

The implication in scripture is that leadership is about equipping the saints for the work of the ministry. Some church structures don't always practise this, but you, in love, still need to move forward.

There is some good news. A few years ago, Gordon MacDonald was asked at a meeting in England what he thought the Church in the future would look like. One of his observations was that historically there has been no bottom line to church leadership – if a leader, for whatever reason, wasn't doing as good a job as perhaps they could, it made no difference whatsoever; they had their job for life. But Gordon MacDonald predicted that this would change. A bottom line *would* come into church leadership, and leaders would either have to respond to the situations around them or lose their positions.

This was said five years ago, and since then I have seen two things start to happen in the Church in Britain. One is that the loyalty of Christians is no longer so strong towards a particular church or denomination. Instead, their loyalty is to God himself and what they feel he has said to them. If churches are a hindrance rather than a help with this, they vote with their feet.

Second, there is a growing trend among Christian leadership of regular evaluation. This evaluation is either imposed by church structures and Christian organisations, or is on a voluntary basis, with leaders subjecting themselves to a thorough evaluation on an annual basis.

'Thorough' can mean that whoever is conducting the evaluation – perhaps another church leader from the area – uses certain criteria to ask the leader's colleagues, and members of his or her congregation, how they feel the leader is doing. The leaders are also asked how they feel they are doing, using the same criteria. This way, the leader gets the opportunity – within, hopefully, a positive, caring situation – to hear the perceptions of colleagues and church members.

Through something like this, leaders can learn how to deal with their weaknesses, either by changing aspects of their leadership style, or by bringing people on to the staff who can complement their weaknesses.

Perhaps in the past we have been afraid to do this, because these leaders are 'the Lord's anointed'. Yes, we do need to respect and honour leaders because we need them to equip and to inspire. At the same time, we need to realise that these are ordinary people who, when it comes to leadership, will inevitably have their strong and weak points.

We need a church culture with a lot more honesty and reality. This can only help everyone in the Church – whether leaders or members – to grow, mature and develop.

Unfulfilled vision and destiny

Many Christians experience disappointment and disillusion-ment because they feel that what God called them to, and the hope they carried in their hearts, never happened. Let us consider three aspects of this.

First, each of us needs to face our own personal responsibilities. Is your vision and destiny unfulfilled because you have not allowed God to do all that he wanted to do in your life? Have you allowed poor theology or personal weakness to triumph?

Second, have you allowed the negative circumstances of your life to shape you far more powerfully than they ought to have done?

Third, has the structure or environment you have belonged in not been conducive to the fulfilment of your vision?

After considering these three aspects, what do you do? Once again, you must return to a dynamic picture of God, and be honest and real with him. It is never too late for God. You can still come to him and say, 'Lord, I feel unfulfilled. I sense there is a vision and destiny in my life that has never happened. Can you still use me for your purpose? Can your redemption still take place in me?'

Redemption is one of the most powerful theological concepts in the New Testament. Redemption means that God is able to step in and change things. I am not talking magic here – what God does may be different from the vision and hope that you have. But God still wants to step in and bring about some positive change.

Have a think about some personal areas in your life. First up is character. Do you have any character weaknesses that have led to sin and made it difficult or impossible for God to do all that he wants with you?

In my early thirties, I went through a make-or-break

situation in Christian ministry. It was becoming clear that even though I had potential in Christian leadership, a great number of people found it difficult to work with me. As a result, I was turned down for a position that I very much wanted. The clouds of disappointment began to gather. At the time, it would have been easy for me to go into victim mentality.

Seeking advice, I went to a colleague of mine called Oliver. I asked him: 'What is it that you find difficult about me?'

After some thought, he answered: 'Laurence, you don't love people.' (I was sure this wasn't right.) Then he explained himself: 'What I mean is, you never listen to people. You express strong opinions, and in so doing, you send out a message that you're more important than others.'

I foolishly went back to my wife and said: 'I've just had this bizarre conversation with Oliver. He says I'm opinion-ated and don't listen to people. What do you think?'

She looked at me as if I had, at this point, gone stark raving mad. 'Laurence, I've been trying to tell you that for years. You never listen to anybody, and your body language can be very unhelpful. When other people and I talk to you, within a few minutes you act like you're bored, and your eyes dart in different directions. But as soon as we say something that is of interest to you, you leap straight into the conversation and take over.'

My wife and others were right. Over the years I had developed unhelpful body language and habits of com-munication. I can honestly say that this was not intentional. I loved my wife. I enjoyed being with the people God had placed me with. Nonetheless, damage was being caused – not only to them, but also in the long term to me.

I had to begin a process where I took ownership of the problem. I did, in one sense, have too high an opinion of my own worth and too low a value of others, and I needed to repent and change.

I also realised that I could learn some little tricks that would help in my communication. One friend taught me some body language I could use to convey that I was listening. Another friend sat next to me in important meetings, and if I began to be too opinionated or show signs that I wasn't listening, they would prod me on the knee under the table. Over a relatively short period of time, I was able to deal with the situation, and a year or so later I was offered the position that I had been turned down for.

Another thing to ask yourself is, are you committed to faithfulness to God, or are you chasing the success syndrome? In today's competitive world, success is the value that drives most people, forcing them to strive to do better. Success brings recognition and security and makes us feel good – or so we think.

The fact is, though, that it rarely does any of those things. It drives people on, and in the end destroys. We have all seen individuals who have been so driven by success that they haven't given the time to their partners and children that they should have. They have also paid the price with ulcers, high blood pressure or heart problems. An increasing number of illnesses today are stress-related, and most of the stress is a result of the success syndrome.

The New Testament encourages a completely different way. God wants to say to us: 'Well done, good and faithful servant' (Matthew 25:21). The key word here is 'faithful'. Your faithfulness shouldn't be measured against anyone else.

Instead, it should be measured against the talents and gifts that you have been given. Faithfulness means asking yourself, 'Am I making the best use of what I have?'

The fact is that there will always be people who are better than you: better parents; better pray-ers; better 'salt and light' missionaries in the workplace; better preachers and teachers; and so on. The moment you compare, you are judging yourself against others. You are beginning to walk under the presence of the clouds.

Here's another question for you: do you have the right expectations of your destiny?

I shall never forget a conversation I had with a man who had had two nervous breakdowns. He told me that a number of years previously he had felt a strong sense of calling, a sense of God speaking to him. He was at the time a journalist, and he really enjoyed his job. But the outcome of his encounter with God was that he believed he should be a church leader. This was what he thought Christian ministry really was.

On two occasions, he pastored churches. On both occasions, he ended up having a nervous breakdown. Finally, he came to the realisation that God had never actually told him to be a pastor. His real gift was writing. He returned to that, and has spent the last ten years working in both the Christian and the secular scene. He is extremely fulfilled, and feels used by God through his gift of writing.

Here is a different story, but with a similar conclusion. I once spoke to a group of lawyers and told them that they were just as much missionaries as I was. They were called to the everyday, marketplace world to be salt and light in their work. In fact, they were probably fighting greater spiritual battles than I would ever fight. I said to them that their role might even be tougher, as to some extent I could measure what I did: messages preached, missionaries sent. How do you measure salt and light? Only by its absence.

As I said this, some of the lawyers began to cry. Two or three of them came up to me afterwards and said, 'Laurence, it's as if we have been living under a cloud. We felt that if we were to be really significant and used by God, we would have to be missionaries like you.'

That day their clouds rolled away, and with renewed enthusiasm they took up their calling to be salt and light in the marketplace.

Disillusionment and disappointment also happens when people allow their self-image to determine what they are going to be and do. What if that self-image is negative?

Around the world – but in British culture especially – we are shaped by negative pictures of ourselves. Deep inside, we feel like failures. We are unworthy.

Perhaps you live with the echo of negative words that were spoken to you ten, twenty or thirty years before – careless words, foolish words, spoken by parents, teachers or friends. You are still haunted by your schooling or social background. People in the past have sown into you a certain perception of who you are and what you can do. You remain locked up, boxed in, never quite fulfilling the destiny that is in you.

In my many years of trying to help people come out of disillusionment and disappointment, there is no greater thrill than when, through a time of counselling, an individual realises that they are not the product of negative words and circumstances. They *are* who God says they are.

A son. A daughter. A prince. A princess. A person with significance, with special gifts, able to make a difference.

> As each has received a gift, employ it for one another, as good stewards of God's varied grace: whoever speaks, as one who utters oracles of God; whoever renders service, as one who renders it by the strength which God supplies; in order that in everything God may be glorified through Jesus Christ.
>
> (1 Peter 4:10–11)

This passage from the New Testament categorically states that all Christians have gifts and graces. Each person might be different, but within each one of us there is something to contribute. You hear of people maximising their potential in a secular career, but inside church these same people sometimes struggle to maximise their potential in the same way.

Perhaps it works a little bit like this. In the workplace, there are two tracks we run on. The first includes promotion, salary and job satisfaction. The other is about fear and bad consequences if we don't perform well. We don't get promoted. We could even lose our job. Ambition – perhaps even fear – drives us. This is why people who are motivated at work normally do well.

However, when it comes to the kingdom of God, whether being salt and light in the workplace or worshipping in a local church, people find it much harder to be motivated. In the kingdom business, there seem to be no tracks. It is far more a case of running on our own motivation, and much of the time there isn't much of that going on.

Perhaps there are two tracks we can work on in the kingdom. The first is having a positive view of ourselves, believing we have a contribution to make. The second is about good stewardship and out of faithfulness fulfilling our responsibilities to the salt and light mandate of the kingdom.

In the parable of the talents that Jesus told, the person who came back with just the one talent unused was not greeted with great affection or 'Well done' by the master. I believe Jesus is implying here that as much as you are loved by God, nevertheless there is an obligation upon you to be a good steward with the gifts you have been given. You need to be driven by faithfulness.

One final note. Your circumstances or environments may not be conducive to your development. In this case, you have to take personal responsibility to do your best. This is all that God is asking from you. Smile at your negative circumstances, and don't let them shape your heart or let the clouds roll over you.

Relationships

As I mentioned earlier, broken relationships can be among the most debilitating experiences in life. *These were my friends; very close friends. But the trust has been broken.*

I am sure just about everyone reading this book has, in one way or another, been affected by a relationship that has gone wrong. Perhaps even today you are still asking the questions: 'Why? What did I do? Why was I treated like this?'

This is one of those areas where the cloud will never totally go away. At best, it may just move from in front of your face, leaving a shadow at your side. Jesus might have asked similar questions: 'Why Peter? Why Judas?'

In this lifetime, you may never know why. There may never be reconciliation, and you may never fully understand. Sometimes you can be so committed to trying to find an answer that it becomes the all-consuming passion and locks you into that hurtful relationship. Perhaps you just have to come to God with honesty and say: 'Yes, God, this hurts. Yes, God, this is not right. But I don't demand an answer. I surrender my right to know.'

Also, the cloud will never move until you release forgiveness.

'Forgive them?' you say. 'You're kidding!'

But the Lord's Prayer is very clear about this – we ask God to forgive our sins, just as we forgive others.

When I talk about forgiveness, I don't mean a feeling. You don't necessarily have to feel good about these people. This is not some unrealistic super-spirituality. This is a conscious choice of your heart and mind that says, 'Just as I have been forgiven my own sins, I choose not to hold this against you.'

Many, if not all, people have been hurt by someone in a way they didn't deserve to be. But for some, that hurt turns into bitterness which ruins their lives. The clouds of bitterness are black and thick. For your own sake, deal with the bitterness before it grows strong. Forgive those who have hurt you. Friends who have let you down. People who have violated you in some way.

Taking courage in your hands, it might also be worth risking an honest conversation with the people involved. Ask if you have done anything to hurt them. It's a risk worth taking. You might be rejected one more time, but you might also find that there has been a misunderstanding. This is your opportunity to sort it out.

Once, a person came to me who felt very hurt and damaged by something I had done many years before. At the heart of this was a misunderstanding, a miscommunication, and in their coming to me resolution and restoration was able to happen.

This is not always the case, but it *can* be. Give God the opportunity to bring healing to your broken relationship.

And keep praying!

Ourselves

Through sin or selfishness, we have perhaps altered the destiny that God had for us.

A few years ago, I talked to a man called George who, in a moment of weakness, had had a sexual dalliance with a seventeen-year-old. When his wife, children and church found out, there were obviously serious consequences. His ministry within a mission agency was over. The new job he was about to be offered within a local church was swiftly withdrawn. He agreed that this was correct, and he knew that he had to go away and spend a number of years working on his relationship with his family and God.

George took me out for lunch one day, and cried when he said, 'Oh, Laurence, if only I hadn't done this. God could be using me right now. Life would be so different.'

In many ways, he felt his life was over. Finished. He could no longer be of use to God, even though he had repented of his sin and sought forgiveness from those involved.

I encouraged him by saying, 'George, your life isn't over. It's just different. I believe that if you are really honest, and right with God and your family, a new day can dawn. God can use you again. You *can* find your ministry, your destiny.'

We looked together at the scriptures that spoke of David's adulterous relationship with Bathsheba, and his subsequent heart-searching and reconciliation with God (see 2 Samuel, chapters 11 and 12). I told George that from this story and many others, I was convinced that God loves us so much that he is the God of the second chance, the third chance, and more.

George left me that day with a new sense of hope. The clouds thinned a little. Today God is using him again, in a different way than before, but nevertheless his sense of purpose and destiny is restored.

Another person I spoke to was a girl called Sarah. Her marriage had broken down, the divorce had come through, and she felt as if her life was in tatters. As far as she was concerned, she had failed big-time, and there was no real future for her, no sense of hope. All she had dreamed of, in terms of evangelism, Christian ministry and being used by God, was over.

We talked, prayed and once again looked at the scriptures. We especially looked at 1 John 1:9 which tells us that 'If we confess our sins, he is faithful and just, and will forgive our sins and cleanse us from all unrighteousness.'

Sarah began to get a sense that perhaps it wasn't over after all – there was the possibility of a new day in Christian ministry. It might be more difficult as being a divorcee is not always acceptable in certain parts of the Church. But she now had a hope, and slowly but surely that hope is turning into a living reality.

You might be disillusioned with work. Remember, though, that however mediocre or boring your workplace is, you go there as an ambassador, as a workplace missionary.

The Apostle Paul talks about us being ambassadors for Christ (2 Corinthians 5:20). Disillusionment can come because we see ourselves as victims of our circumstances. But one way of finding hope is to see that in God's economy, it's not just a matter of whether you enjoy work, have nice work colleagues, are paid the sort of money you ought to be paid, or have the career opportunities you think you ought to have. Yes, it would be great if you did, but God's encouragement is that through taking your love for the lost to work as a marketplace missionary, you have purpose.

You might be in a position of seniority in your company. Slowly, over a period of time, you could change the landscape in your workplace. You have the power to rearrange the big picture and bring Christian values to your company.

Many people won't have that kind of authority, but you can still make a difference on a smaller scale. Thinking of your workplace, if you cannot change the whole 'scene', you might be able to change a little bit of it. The way you respond, the way you treat people in your everyday life, can bring about the kingdom of God. Be encouraged, therefore, that if your workplace is a dark place, as you step into that darkness as an ambassador of God, whether you feel it or not, you have authority. Thinking about it this way, you are no longer a victim. Instead, you are a worker for the kingdom of God.

But what will drive you as God's ambassador? Remind yourself not to live in the world's value system. If you allow success to drive you, if you measure yourself against others, you will be depressed. God isn't asking you to be successful. He wants you to be faithful with the talent that you have. That is all.

Billy Graham was once asked what he attributed his great success to. His reply was: 'I have never sought to be successful, only faithful – to be as good an evangelist as I can possibly be.' Billy Graham never tried to be a great man, only a faithful man.

As far as the treatment of women is concerned, there is no doubt that society, and even the Church, has much to answer for. How can you work with God to change this environment? And for those women who are living in the reality of disillusionment, how can their cloud move so that they feel the Son?

Our world needs to discover God's truth about gender equality. Both a woman and a man were created in order to fully and accurately reflect the image of God. Both were created to illustrate the community of the Godhead. And both were given the responsibility to reproduce and take dominion over creation. When this truth is embraced by females and males alike, hope can begin to take the place of disillusionment.

In large parts of western society, we are already seeing a change. Many countries are improving their laws relating to women in the workplace. The situation is more positive generally.

Unfortunately, there are still times when the Church and family life cause pain and disillusionment for many women. The first step in dealing with this is to be a lot more honest. To say, 'Yes, we have treated women poorly, but we want to see and do things differently.'

We also need to ask ourselves some challenging questions. As parents, do we esteem and respect our daughters, encouraging their hopes and dreams as much as our sons? As husbands, do we respect and honour our wives? As mothers, do we help our daughters appreciate and value their femininity by how we live ourselves? As fathers, do we model love and respect for women to our sons?

Even when women have fully embraced their true worth and identity, living this out in a 'man's world' is still extremely challenging. Support from other women who are on a similar journey can be very encouraging and liberating. Support from the significant men in their lives, either in the family or workplace, can also be a big help.

One way you can provide support is by allowing women the 'space' to be who they are as women – to function as women would. In other words, it is no more fair to expect a woman to conform to a man's way of doing things than to expect a man to conform his ways to those of a woman.

'Space' must be made for both genders to be fully who they are as female and male – in the family, in the Church, and in the work environment.

There is hope when it comes to our children as well. Remember, we do not live in a closed environment. Love and prayer can and do change things. God can step in. We hear story after story of children whose lives have been horrendously damaged by themselves or others, and who have caused their parents great grief – yet change can still come. What we see is only half the reality. The other half is what we pray and hope for.

Parents need to resist the feeling of condemnation. No parent is perfect, and you cannot afford to live with a sense of failure. If you have failed in some areas, say sorry. Whether it is received or not, the important thing for you is to apologise. Sometimes things have happened that are no fault of the parents at all. Don't allow yourself to be separated from God's love or the possibility of hope.

A number of years ago, Gerald Coates was asked the same question Billy Graham was asked: what was the secret of his success? Gerald answered with: 'I have failed many times. I have fallen over many times. But I always got up again.'

Here is your challenge. No matter what your circumstances might be, and however you feel you have succeeded or failed, believe a few simple things: you *are* who God says you are; you *can* do what God says you can do; there *is* forgiveness and cleansing; and you *can* begin anew.

Whether your circumstances are of your own making, or you are the victim of them, there is always the possibility of a brand new day.

7

'Where is God in All This?'

In our time of crisis, our family found God in five different ways:

1   God was with us by the Spirit, and we communicated with him through prayer.
2   God was with us through his word – i.e. through scripture. Biblical truths and principles are more than just wise words; they have within them the presence of God. As we seek to live by them and put them into practice, they have power to bring change.
3   God was in the body. A strong New Testament picture is of the Church being the body of Christ. As Christians reach out to each other through sacrificial love, something of the presence of God, which enables that sacrifice, flows through those human acts of hospitality, kindness and care.
4   God was found through the Church, in its many sacraments – such as prayer, worship, the breaking of bread, or communion – as well as the laying on of hands.
5   We also found God through obedience to the prompting of the Holy Spirit and obedience to biblical principles.

I hope that, from our personal story of how we met God in the hard times, you will see how these various principles were at work. We found strength in the midst of our particular crisis and difficulty. You can as well.

As the situation with Justyn deteriorated, and he became increasingly violent and difficult, we became more desperate as we tried to cope. As a result, several quite natural factors came into play. One was our discovery that if you feel emotionally alienated and damaged in one area of your life, these feelings affect every other area. Automatically, God feels far away, as if he doesn't care. Of course this is not true, but it is still a very real feeling.

Prayer

The first lesson we learned was to keep on praying. A number of years before our difficulty with Justyn took place, Ailish and I made a commitment to spend five or ten minutes in prayer together most days, and this was a habit pattern that had been well formed and shaped. When the difficulties arose, it was therefore quite natural to spend five or ten minutes every morning crying out to God. Sometimes with anger, sometimes with tears, sometimes pleading, but always talking.

As month followed month, it appeared that there weren't any major answers forthcoming. But looking back, we can see that our prayers *were* answered. Even in the worst days, we had strength to face the next day. Eventually, through practical and medical help, and through spiritual accountability, the answers came.

I am convinced that this daily discipline was the lifeline

that kept our faith intact. For many months it felt as though we were on our own, talking to ourselves. But that feeling was the result of our own limited emotions. The fact was that God was there and he was always at work in the situation.

God is with us by the Spirit. Our prayer and conversations with him take us out of the world of 'reality' – the world of touch and feel – into the world of the Spirit where our requests to God have impact. We may not feel that God is there and listening, but our faith says that he *is* there.

Almost despite myself, I began to feel the presence of God in new ways. Jesus became alive to me, and my passion for him was re-awoken.

Many years before, I had gone to Australia as an unconverted, very conceited and fairly arrogant young man. While there, I gave my life to Christ and became a 'Jesus freak'. This was an interesting experience, to say the least. Much of what I did lacked wisdom, but there was also a passion for Christ.

Before the difficulties with Justyn, I re-visited Australia and had the opportunity to return to the street corner where I gave my life to Christ.

When I came back, I had a conversation with Ken McGreavy, a colleague of mine. Ken said to me: 'We begin our Christian lives with an enthusiasm and passion for Jesus. Then we move into a phase of learning the principles and ways of God, which is often seen as Christian maturity.'

But Ken pointed out that many people lose their passion for Jesus during this time, and often get caught up in cold, old, dry principles. Real maturity comes from passion and principle working together.

I realised that, slowly but surely, the situation with Justyn had forced me back to my roots. Was Jesus really going to be the centre of my life? To my amazement, for both Ailish and me a new passion for Jesus was emerging in the midst of pain and difficulty. Jesus was becoming more real to us.

We had both had many fantastic spiritual experiences in years past, but this experience seemed to be of different stuff. I began to notice that when I spoke or preached – even though I felt damaged and frail, sometimes cried, and found it hard to continue speaking – God was using my pain and speaking through it. An underlying, deeper, more powerful spiritual reality was emerging in my life.

Another aspect of meeting with God by the Spirit is to believe that we are filled with the Holy Spirit; Acts 1:8 says we will receive power to be a witness. This word 'witness' takes its root from the word 'martyr', about laying our lives down. It is implying that our underlying witness is not just the words we speak to people, it is the lives we live, and we can call upon God through the power of the Holy Spirit to help us.

A friend once explained it like this: we can be a thermometer Christian, whose Christian life goes up and down according to the experiences we are going through, or we can be a thermostat Christian – someone who is plugged into a source of power that is released to change the environment.

Through our prayer times, and indeed through the other ways that Ailish and I met with God, we were in a sense many times calling out to God for the power of the Holy Spirit, knowing that our own resources were wholly inadequate: we only had the resources to be a thermometer

Christian. As we cried out to God on a daily basis for power, for grace, it is not that the problems disappeared, or that we had incredible mystical experiences – indeed, for much of the time the problems got worse and the pain was harder; nonetheless, throughout it there was a sense that God was with us by the Spirit. Indeed, over a long period of time, one can see the work of the Holy Spirit through all sorts of ways and circumstances.

I have outlined many principles which we need to put in place, but as we do this, we are looking to God through the power of the Holy Spirit to have an impact on our lives.

The word

The second place we met God was through the Bible. Christians believe that the Bible is far more than just a collection of fantastic sayings and principles. In some strange way, words in scripture are not just ordinary words, but God-words. Scripture is breathed on by God and there is spiritual life in its words and principles.

But what about the times when it's difficult to read the Bible? It's not that you don't respect what the scriptures say, but the emotional damage that you carry makes it very hard.

We found two contradictory experiences. One is that, for the first time in our Christian lives, we realised that at this particular time we didn't *have* to read the Bible every day; it was too difficult, and we found that we could meet God in other means which I outline in this chapter. But on the other hand, we found ourselves resting on the historical Bible reading that we had done. We found, as you can imagine, that some of the good old faithful passages, such as Psalm 23, became very meaningful. Rather than reading new material, we would go back to those favourite passages and allow those verses to reassure us.

Ailish and I did find it hard, but we learnt many things through trying to be faithful with our reading. One of the major lessons we learnt from the scriptures was that God lives in the body of Christ, among his believers.

The body

A story we read in the Old Testament told of David when he was really thirsty. He mentioned in the hearing of some of his men that he would love to have some water from a particular well, which at that time was in enemy territory. So his men, at risk to their own lives, fought their way to the place where the well was and brought some of the water back to David.

On receiving this gift, rather than drinking it, he declared that the water was holy and poured it on the ground. The sacrifice of his men had somehow made it holy. A similar principle is at work with the sacrifices of the body of Christ to each other.

Another phenomenon you might face is the sense of alienation from others – a feeling of being alone because nobody understands what you are going through. It might be tempting, but if you cut yourself off from other Christians, it will be more difficult for you to meet with God. To overcome this, you need to have a strategy in your mind.

For Ailish and me, there were two things that were amazingly important in helping us, even though at the time they did not appear to be. First, we made a decision to be open and honest with our pastor, as well as a small group of six or seven close personal friends. As mentioned in a previous chapter, I asked them if I could send them a monthly newsletter for their prayers. The letter also acted as a means by which I could let out some of the pain and difficulty.

At the time this was very difficult to do, and some of the advice we received was that we should keep very quiet about the situation to protect my position. But over the next two years, some of the most uplifting and encouraging ways we met with God were through the friendship of others.

One thing I did at this time was cut back on preaching and teaching engagements, but this immediately affected our income. At just the right time, a friend rang to ask about our income, and he was moved to put a cheque for £4,000 in the post that very day. As you can imagine, this was a huge weight lifted. We had enough battles to fight just to survive, without worrying about money as well.

I've already told of a friend who rang us on a particularly awful Christmas Day, with the amazing impact and hope that this produced. Time and time again, God came to us in the form of his people.

By the summer of the year that Justyn had blown up, Ailish and I were at the point of spiritual and emotional exhaustion. Our two daughters were also showing signs of pain and distress. We were still in shock from the aftermath of Justyn's suicide attempt, and we desperately needed a break.

Around this time, a colleague in YWAM – Andy Kennedy of the children's ministry King's Kids – got in touch. He said that he would take Justyn for two weeks on a King's

Kids programme, which Justyn wanted to do. We explained to Andy how difficult this might be, as Justyn was fine on some days and totally out of control on others. Nonetheless, Andy took Justyn on the two-week programme, and we went on holiday and had two weeks of rest. This was a big blessing from God.

Another friend wrote to us, enclosing a pamphlet describing something called Attention Deficit Hyperactivity Disorder, or ADHD for short. This was something we had never heard of, and we bought some books to find out more. As we read them, we were staggered to find that the material described Justyn in perfect detail. Not only this, the books gave clues to certain possible solutions.

What Ailish and I learned from all this was to take help from wherever it came from, to be accountable, and also to be prepared to change.

I mentioned in Chapter 1 that Ailish and I were referred to Social Services and the specialised family unit run by the local council. This was unbearably humiliating, to sit in a room with two professionals, knowing that there was a glass screen with two or three more people behind it observing us. Our lives were examined from birth to the present moment, with somewhat unpleasant facts pointed out to us.

There was an overwhelming desire to escape, to run away. But we had to keep going to these sessions. If we didn't, we knew that the authorities were within their rights to take Justyn from us, or to do whatever they considered appropriate.

It didn't take the professionals long to point out that we weren't in control of our family – that, in fact, Justyn was the controlling point. It also wasn't long before I became the focus of their work, where they quizzed me and firmly pointed out that my abstract, laid-back approach to fatherhood, my non-confrontational nature, and my slow but sure undermining of Ailish's authority, was, in their opinion, a major contributing factor to Justyn's problems.

And what was I going to do about it?

Since the beginning of the difficulties with Justyn, I had started to meet on a regular basis with a mature Christian friend and leader, called Iain. At the same time, I placed myself under the care of a psychologist to try to unravel the difficulty. Out of this came the understanding of the Harrods syndrome and the fact that I needed to draw boundaries. Naturally, I confided in Iain, and he held me spiritually accountable to this, checking up on me at regular times to see how I was doing. It was as though he was my spiritual director.

Writing this now, in black and white, makes it all seem like a clinical, straightforward process. But at the time it was hell on earth. Having to face my inadequacies, to take some responsibility for my part in what had taken place, and to really be prepared to do something about it, was extremely hard. To be honest, if there had been any way of avoiding it, I would have done. But making myself accountable to Christian leadership was one of the things that pushed me forward.

We also got in touch with a private paediatrician who was one of the few people at the time prepared to diagnose ADHD. It took four months to get an appointment, and cost us a lot of money. Once again, some wonderful friends stepped in and paid the medical bill.

When the appointment eventually came round, Justyn was in the foulest of moods. His hyperactivity was at an extreme level, and he was very aggressive. After some testing, the paediatrician confirmed our suspicions – Justyn did have ADHD. It was recommended that we put Justyn on a drug called Ritalin. We didn't know at the time that this was a very controversial treatment.

We were told that within twenty minutes of taking the medicine, Justyn would calm down. The hyperactivity would ebb away. He would then be able to concentrate, and he ought to use the drug at school. There would be times at home when he would not be on the Ritalin and we would need to use the techniques we were being taught by the family therapy unit. I would need to continue to draw boundaries and stand up to Justyn.

So, after eight months of real pressure and difficulty, we were about to see the first breakthrough. As controversial as Ritalin might be, in Justyn's case the results were nothing short of miraculous. In the previous eight months, we had been in almost weekly contact with the school, who were dealing as best as they could with Justyn's hyperactivity and daily disruptive attitude.

After six months of this treatment, we went to the school to find out about Justyn's academic abilities. We had previously been told that he had an IQ of about 75, was totally ineducable, and would end up either in prison or in care. There were other, equally discouraging pronouncements.

But this time, teacher after teacher showed us Justyn's work before and after Ritalin. All of them said words to the effect of: 'What happened? Justyn is a different boy. Last year our opinion was that he would never pass a GCSE, and that we were all in for four or five long hard years with him. But the quality of work that Justyn is beginning to develop is of GCSE standard, and while his behaviour is still difficult, it is getting better week by week.'

A miracle!

We had learned, in many different ways, that asking for help and being prepared to do something about it enabled us to take an impossible situation and make it possible.

God is in the body. We are not designed as Christians to make it on our own. Being an active part of the body of Christ, with giving and receiving, should be a vital part of your Christian life.

Church

Going to church can also be difficult in these times. For us, it was often just the very practical difficulty of taking Justyn along. How would he behave?

For many people, though, it is the sheer tenderness of one's feelings and emotions. Worship, at least in my experience, touches your emotions. If they are raw, this is not always a very easy or pleasant experience. For no apparent reason, you begin to cry and feel very awkward in this public place.

Ailish and I realised that although the temptation to abandon church was very great, we needed to do the exact opposite: to go to more meetings, and make ourselves vulnerable by asking for prayer.

So we began a phase of our life where Ailish and I went to many meetings, and we always went forward when there was an opportunity to be prayed for or ministered to. This was during the time of the Toronto Blessing, so there were plenty of opportunities. Everybody was offering prayer!

Week after week we would go forward for prayer, but nothing much happened. Many times we felt that God was as far away as he had ever been. We weren't falling over like everyone else, and we didn't feel blessed by God.

Nonetheless, something *was* happening. We were learning to place ourselves in an attitude of receiving, which is very hard when you are going through times of difficulty.

One of the traditional ways of receiving is through communion. Jesus commanded us to take of the bread and the wine in remembrance of him. However your tradition delivers communion, whether it is going forward to an altar, kneeling and lifting up your hands or whether it is passing the elements to one another along a row, there is something very special in partaking of the bread and the wine. As we take the bread, we are saying that we are a part of the body of Christ. There is a picture here that the people who are standing around us are sharing in our difficulties, but more particularly this is about a broken body, and Jesus himself both understands and has shared in our pain and our suffering. Through the wine we are affirming the promises. The wine is the sign of the covenant that was the blood of Jesus and this means that all his promises are true. He is with us. The physical discipline of taking communion is an opportunity for our tired and battered souls to be confronted by a greater truth that God has died to give us strength and grace to go through.

Similarly, some of your churches will give you the opportunity to have hands laid on you. This is perhaps more familiar in some new churches. We allowed people to pray for us and lay hands on us many times, and even though we did not necessarily have huge experiences, we realised that this attitude of receiving, this asking to be prayed for, this taking of communion, had, over a period of two years, had a powerful impact. We could look back and say yes, we had received. But it could not be defined in any one moment or any one occasion; just the cumulative effect of doing the right thing, of placing ourselves in the institution of Church, had a restorative effect.

This receiving attitude is a very important part of our understanding of how the kingdom of God works. In our relationship with God and with others, giving and receiving is a dynamic principle. Some people are natural givers; some are natural receivers. But you need to be both.

The New Testament is filled with the teaching that we are the body of Christ, and that God lives in his body. The implication of this is that sometimes when we do what appear to be very human things – such as offer help, phone a friend with words of encouragement, give sacrificially to people or be available for them – these human activities become channels for the presence of God because *we* are the body of Christ. God encourages, strengthens and enables people through the love that has been expressed through fellow Christians.

Obedience

Perhaps one of the hardest yet one of the simplest things for us to comprehend is that God is *in* our obedience. As you obey the leading of the Spirit and the principles of scripture, God gives you power. You can talk to God every day, you can read the Bible regularly, you can get involved in church, you can have hands laid on you or take communion. But none of this is worth too much if you aren't prepared to be obedient, seeking to submit your will to the things you know God is saying to you.

Jesus said: 'If you love me, you will keep my commandments' (John 14:15).

The Apostle John writes: 'walk in the light, as he is in the light' (1 John 1:7).

Throughout scripture there is the explicit challenge that, as best you are able, and with faltering and weak steps, you need to obey what God has said to you and the principles that scripture and others have made clear.

For me, this was about cutting back the amount of time I spent travelling to speak and teach. This was so that I could spend more time with my family. I realised that in the years to come, I would not be able to reclaim this time. Obedience also meant learning to parent in a different way.

Obedience will mean different things to each one of us. The danger we need to be aware of is that sometimes we look for the 'God, God, God' solution, where everything begins with God. *He* does all the work and gets all the glory.

'God, God, God' solutions sound admirable, but they seldom happen. In reality, it is more a 'God, us, God' solution. He has made the first move, and you need to think about how you can then co-operate with him, putting your will behind what he is saying. God still gets the glory, because there is very little you can do without his grace and the empowering of his Spirit.

So, where is God? Christians believe that he is with us because we have asked him to be. Whether we feel him or not, he is committed to us.

He is in the scriptures. When scriptural principles are applied to your life, when you act on them as if they are truth, and when you believe the promises of his presence and help, they are there.

Lastly, God is in the body. In times of pain and disillusionment, praying and being a member of a church is hard going, and reading the Bible is sometimes impossible. But one of the places God seems to turn up the most is through his body – our friends and spiritual leaders. If we cut ourselves off from these people, it is at our own expense, and we are blocking one of the ways that God wants to help us.

In times of difficulty, as the advert says, keep on talking. Keep praying, regardless of how you are feeling. If the Bible is hard to read, keep reading!

Do what you know is right, and you can still meet with God in the hard times.

8

Spiritual Disciplines

When we think of spiritual disciplines, our minds jump to the things we think we ought to be doing: prayer times, Bible reading, church attendance, making the right decisions.

There has been a lot of emphasis in modern Christianity on 'doing', involving our actions and our wills. In this chapter I want to explore another way of looking at spiritual disciplines.

One of the key 'change' words in the New Testament is 'repent' (see Acts 3:19, for example). If you ask people what they think you mean by this, most will say that it is an action, a change in direction, a conscious choice that they need to make. But the Greek word that is translated 'repent' means 'to change the mind'.

What I want to look at in this chapter are the values that underline the actions and choices you will make – values that will help you 'change the mind'.

A hundred years ago, many of the values of Christianity were also the values of society in general. This is why back then Christians majored on challenging people's wills, urging them to repent. Today, the values of society – the way people think about each other, love, honesty, a whole bunch of things – are very different. The western world has departed a great deal from Christian values, which means that a different set of spiritual disciplines is needed.

We are not the first group of people to face this challenge. In the first three centuries of the Christian Era, the values of the world were pagan. The early Church, in disciplining new believers, worked on three concepts in their catechism process: beliefs or values; belonging; and behaviour.

They realised that for people's behaviour to change, they must first have the right value system: they needed to see God in a new and dynamic way; they needed to understand others and love them in a new and positive way; they needed to have a different picture of themselves; and they needed to have a different view of the world they lived in, as well as understanding their responsibilities in it.

I see these values as foundations – the rocks on which we stand.

> Every one then who hears these words of mine and does them will be like a wise man who built his house upon the rock; and the rain fell, and the floods came, and the winds blew and beat upon that house, but it did not fall, because it had been founded on the rock.
>
> (Matthew 7:24–5)

Many of the letters of Paul, and indeed the teachings of Jesus, encourage us to think of foundations. But the story of the house built on the rock in Matthew 7 is also about the storms that are to come.

Build spiritual disciplines in your life now before troubles come. You can be absolutely certain that when difficulties come flooding in, you will not have the time or inclination to be out there building foundations. The sooner you build some spiritual disciplines in your life, the better your foundations will be.

This is not a very attractive concept in the twenty-first century. The word 'discipline' in any shape or form is seen as negative. Perhaps the term 'spiritual foundations' is more attractive. Whatever way you look at it, you need foundations.

So often, people try to deal with the world of actions and choices, but the real battle is in your mind with your value systems. A line of consequential behaviour might look like this:

Beliefs → Values → Actions → Habits → Character

Who you are is displayed in your character. In a sense, your character is made up of your habit patterns and spiritual disciplines – or maybe even your lack of them.

Your habits are there because of your actions. As mentioned before, any action that is repeated thirty-two to sixty-four times becomes a habit pattern, or automatic behaviour. It is a building block in your character.

As you build on the rock, on Christ, you have to ensure that your beliefs and values are the *right* beliefs and values. These will enable you to have good habits in your life, and therefore Christian character.

The Apostle Paul picks this up in Romans when he talks about the renewed mind:

Do not be conformed to this world but be transformed by the renewal of your mind, that you may prove what is the will of God, what is good and acceptable and perfect.

(Romans 12:2)

As you can see, Paul is also saying that you can know what the will, or mind, of God is: that which is good, acceptable and perfect.

Consider this some more. Christians often have the right beliefs. They believe in God. They believe that Jesus is God's Son, and that he was sent by God for their redemption so that they can be forgiven and cleansed, and come into relationship with God through Christ. These are good beliefs. But belief isn't enough. It needs to work its way through to a different area: your value system.

I have seen so many Christians trying to cope with life by using the wrong value system. In my own story, I was trying to do the right things, but in my heart and mind I had the wrong value system.

Don't use the world's value system. A crucial spiritual discipline is examining your value system and, if it is out of kilter, allowing God to change it.

The character and nature of God

There are a number of areas in your life where you need to have the right beliefs and values. First, and most important, is your view of God. How do you see him?

Sometimes when a Christian tells you what he or she thinks God is like, you realise that they have a distorted view of God's character. It might be that their circumstances and background have shaped their picture of God.

This can be illustrated by using the first line of the Lord's Prayer. Jesus tells us to pray in terms of 'Our Father', which could also be translated as 'Our Daddy', a very intimate phrase. For many people, though, this is not a helpful image. A father could have been a figure of abuse, a person who abandoned them, or someone who was passive and absent when it came to his children. Many people find it extremely hard to think of God as Father in a positive light.

To get a true picture of God, you need to be spiritually disciplined and examine the biblical picture. What does God say about himself in scripture? What has he demonstrated? What is his track record? And so on. You can then form a picture from what you have read.

Scripture portrays God as love. This love is ultimately manifested in God giving up his own Son Jesus, with Christ dying on the cross for us.

Also, when God calls himself Father, he is not just aligning himself to the masculine view of this word. Genesis tells us that humans – male *and* female – are made in the image of God. God has the capacity for all of the tenderness and affection normally attributed to women, and the strength and action normally attributed to men.

One of the most important foundations you can build in your life for the future – whether it holds good times or bad times – is to have right thinking about God. This includes dealing with the very difficult subject of his interaction with humankind.

Why her?

Some months ago I was asked by a friend to visit a young couple whose two-year-old daughter had been found dead in her cot. They were still stunned and haunted by the old question Why? and sometimes, Why her? I simply could not offer the parents the conventional reassurance about it all being in God's providence, a mystery now but one day to be seen as part of a loving plan. I know that many good souls derive lasting comfort from such counsel, and it certainly squares with a good deal in the Bible, and is to be found in many books of devotion and pastoral practice. But to me it has become unconvincing and suggests a picture of God I find impossible to love, arrogant though that sounds. I said to them instead that their child's death was tragic, far from being planned by God, it was for him a disaster and frustration of his will for life and fulfilment, just as it was for them, that God shared their pain and loss and was with them in it. I went on to say that God is not a potentate ordering this or that to happen, but that the world is full of chance and accident, and God has let it be so because that is the one sort of world in which freedom, development, responsibility and love could come into being, but that God was committed to this kind of a world in love and to each person in it, and was with them in this tragedy, giving himself to them in fortitude, healing and faith to help them through. And their child was held in that same caring, suffering love.

In this quote by Bishop John V. Taylor, from his book *Weep Not For Me*,[4] you see a fantastic theological tension: because humankind has been given the tremendous gift of love, we are free agents.

Unless you are truly free, you cannot truly love. If everything was determined or controlled, you would just be a sophisticated animal. Humankind has this capacity to live beyond programming because we are free. But in creating freedom, there is the inevitable pain that is caused by the abuse of that freedom.

Having created freedom, God has also made available his presence for those who call upon his name. He will step back into the pain and difficulty that falls upon the just and the unjust, the Christian and the non-Christian, and will give them grace and strength to live through it.

Many more pages and chapters could be written on having a biblical view of God. It is vitally important. Also important is maintaining this view. Doubts will appear, needs will arise, situations will happen that will cause your picture of God to be shaken. This is when you will need to fall back on your foundations – your basic spiritual disciplines.

The value of others

We have looked at how we view God. A second thing to examine is how we view others. What value do we place on other human beings? In my own case, I freely admit that this was an area where my value system was far from good. But I wasn't the only one. Again and again, I see Christians treating people in a way that shows they don't have a biblical value system.

In 2 Corinthians we read that Christ died for all. This

tells us something of the value of every human being. We are also commanded to no longer be self-seeking, but instead think of God and of others.

> And he died for all, that those who live might live no longer for themselves, but for him who for their sake died and was raised.
>
> (2 Corinthians 5:15)

At the heart of Christianity is a very profound and simple truth: every human being, from whatever race, and whether rich or poor, is of immense value. God gave his only Son, and Christ died for all. Humans are the beneficiaries of this sacrificial love.

This profound truth has a twist in its tale. Christians must be controlled or ruled by this value. In other words, they now have to see everybody differently.

The difficult neighbour, the trying Christian, the victim on the television, everyone you know – they all have to be loved by you because of their value and intrinsic worth. This kind of love and motivation isn't necessarily emotionally fired. It should come from a profound change in your mind and heart.

When I was younger I did some work in a Christian outreach centre. One day, a little boy strolled in, smelling of urine and excrement. He rushed straight up to me, with his arms outstretched, waiting to be loved and hugged. I confess that I failed this little boy. I couldn't hug him. All I could think of was the urine and excrement, and my emotions did not respond with the love that he needed.

That night in my prayers, I learned an important lesson.

Real Christian love isn't powered by emotions, but by a change in perspective. When I prayed and saw this boy from God's perspective, I realised that in this case love was not a feeling, but a change of values producing different actions. The next time this little boy rushed in, by the grace of God I could hug and hold him.

The world is full of pain, and it needs the body of Christ to hug and hold it. Your love should be truly evangelistic. In other words, love kept at home makes no difference. Perhaps this is why the New Testament is so strong on the gift of hospitality. Hospitality, that forgotten command of the New Testament, is surely love in action.

If your value system is not right when it comes to other people, in the end you will not treat your colleagues at work, your friends at home, your wife, husband or children, in the way that you should. You will store up for yourself problems and difficulties.

A common source of pain is the breakdown of human relationships. This largely happens through people not having a high enough view of love or people. Because of this, they indirectly or directly treat others in a way that will eventually cause pain and difficulty. When a husband or a wife treats their partner as an object, as someone who has a function, they abuse the rights and privileges of love. Slowly but surely, pain will arise and that relationship will die.

Be aware that this spiritual discipline needs to be on-going. You may have one or two life-changing moments where you glimpse God's heart for people and begin to love in a new, dynamic way, but this could soon fade. You need to continually take on board these values, year by year, month by month, resolving to see people as they really are –

as God sees them – and endeavouring to treat them accordingly.

The value of yourself

You also need to see yourself as you really are.

The sad fact is that in the world at large, many people suffer from a negative picture of themselves. This includes Christians. They hear a persistent whisper from their past that says they are nothing, they can achieve nothing and their life has no merit. These feelings of inadequacy and negativity rule their lives.

When people feel negative about themselves this stops the body of Christ being as dynamic as it ought to be. It stops the Church being the healing community that it should be. There is so much potential locked up in people's lives. So many good gifts of love, kindness, hospitality and prayer that are never expressed because individuals do not think well enough of themselves for God to use them.

God wants you to be a good steward of the resources he has given you. Part of your love for God is to believe that you *are* who he says you are – that you *can* do what he says you can do. He is calling you to live beyond the 'I can't', to the 'I can.' To live beyond 'I don't have a contribution to make', to 'I *do* have a contribution.' To live beyond the isolation of gender – whether you are male or female, you *can* achieve and do all that God wants you to.

I have already mentioned that many women have a negative self-image, partly because of the belief and culture system of Church. It is often harder for a woman to have confidence in herself, to believe that she can really make a contribution, because of these negative messages that Church and society send out.

It is interesting to note that my personal observation has been that many women who have achieved great things in life came from all-girls schools where they had formidable headmistresses. These headmistresses believed that 'their gals' could achieve anything, go anywhere. Remarkably, that often became the case, largely because a positive value had been placed inside them.

You may not have received that kind of positive reinforcement, so you must – from scripture and your Christian faith – find a positive picture that allows you to change your view of yourself.

You can also do this for others. As part of your spiritual discipline, be a person who speaks worth into the lives of others – into your children, friends, family and colleagues. Treat them and speak to them in ways that leave them believing they are of real worth and value.

The value of the material world

Finally, you need to reassess how you view the material world. Christians can cause themselves a lot of pain by their handling of finances, accumulation of material things and their view of the world at large. This is not an area that is often addressed in Christian circles, but nonetheless it is important to have some values in place as part of your spiritual discipline.

One of the messages of the material world is: 'Consume as much as you can, spend all that you have, and enjoy all of the world's delights and possibilities.' The sad truth, as pointed out by Christian thinkers like Tom Sine, is that often there is very little difference between the Christians and the non-Christians. Christians spend their money on the same things, and have very similar lifestyles.

One of the things we need to look at here is stewardship. The teaching of Jesus shows that stewardship is for the whole of your life, and not just related to money and possessions. It means your talents in terms of gifts and ministry skills, your time, and yes, your resources. Your value system here should tell you that you are not the owner and controller, but you have given everything to God, and he has entrusted it back into your hands.

Now, what does this mean in practice? Does it mean that you cannot spend money on yourself, or that you cannot experience some of the luxuries of life? I don't think it says that. To me, it's all about generosity. As a spiritual discipline, God is looking for the value of generosity in your life as it relates to your time, your skills and your resources.

Sometimes, people limit their lifestyles so that they have resources to give and be generous with. You can see this in the present-day Mennonite communities, as well as in the lives of John Wesley and other great Christian heroes.

In a sense, though, this limitation is a personal choice. Sometimes, it's okay to be well-off. Scripture encourages rich people to be generous.

I know of a couple who live in what most of us would consider a top-of-the-range house, with five or six acres of gardens. It would be tempting to judge them as materialistic.

But I happen to know that many years ago they decided to give away the money that would have been spent on a butler, a private helicopter, a yacht, their house in Paris, and so on – and over the years they have given literally millions of pounds to the work of the kingdom of God.

Similarly, I know of many young people who have also made sacrifices, such as deciding to drink two fewer pints of beer each week and giving that money to student mission.

Whether you are rich or not-so-rich, generosity is a foundational value in the kingdom of God. Think about it. Creation itself is the most extravagant act of generosity ever. Not one star, but millions. Not one type of flower, but countless varieties. Also, God was so generous to us that he gave his only Son.

The New Testament emphasises being hospitable as a qualification of spiritual leadership. Hospitality is an aspect of generosity, but on a practical level. If you understand evangelism as a dynamic relational process, the whole area of being hospitable becomes more and more important. It might just be inviting people in for a cup of tea.

In today's world, Christian and non-Christian alike are initially more interested in who you are and the way you live your life rather than the truth you might have for them. This is not to downplay the significance of truth. Truth is important, but it must be communicated through your relationships.

So, spiritual disciplines are crucial, and the most important discipline is the renewing of your mind and a change in your underlying values.

If you see God in the right way, it will inspire your prayer life, your personal relationship with God, and your reading of his word.

If you see people in the right way, it will inspire your evangelism, and your wanting to be a part of the body of Christ.

If you see yourself in the right way, you will realise that your contribution is vital – that you have something to offer in your own church, your community, and in your work-place.

If you see material things in the right way, not only do you get the opportunity to enjoy some of the goodness of God's creation, you can also play a part in resourcing God's work.

9

Preparing for Tomorrow's Pain and Disillusionment

The best time to deal with pain, trouble and disillusionment, is *before* it happens. Then, when the unexpected comes along, you will have enough foundations in your life to sustain you.

We have already looked at prayer, right thinking and positive practical theology. In this chapter I want to explore some of the relational dynamics you will need to have in place. These principles are designed to help if difficulties arise, but they also put principles into your life which might prevent one or two things actually developing into major problems.

Friendships

Friendship is one of the greatest gifts you can have and give – spending time with a person, or a group of people, who don't just love you in the esoteric or Christian sense, but actually like you. You enjoy being in their company, they enjoy being in your company, they accept your strengths and weaknesses, and there is an unspoken commitment that in the good times and the bad times you will stand with and care for one another.

It may only be a handful of people, and they may or may not be in your church. But they will be people you see regularly enough for your relationship with them to have meaning and strength.

Fifteen years ago, in the midst of a hectic schedule of hyper Christian activity, I felt God speak to me to make some friends. I had some great colleagues and a wonderful wife, but few real friends.

Initially, my dialogue with God was: *I can't. I'm too busy. I'm too this, I'm too that.* But after a while, I gave in. I realised that this was a genuine prompting of God, and I needed to do something about it.

Then and there, I prayed, 'God, over the next few years, show me the people I need to be friends with. People who can be encouraged and helped by friendship with me, and vice versa.'

Over the next five to ten years, this prayer was answered. I came in touch with a number of people – sometimes through my wife – that I realised I needed to make friends with.

Making friends is one of those things that doesn't just happen. It takes commitment, sacrifice and time, and a certain amount of vulnerability. You might ask someone round for a meal, and it's a risk. *Will they turn up? What will happen? Will it be a disaster?* But having made a commitment to make friends, you need to follow this through.

Here's your choice: do you allow your life to rule and shape you, or do you rule and shape your life? You might even have to sit down with your diary and say, 'I will invite this couple round for a meal. I will go and play golf with Joe. I will ring Jane on Tuesday night.'

Slowly but surely, acquaintance turns into friendship. It doesn't happen every time, but sometimes you know that this relationship has now become important in and of itself.

How can you tell the difference between a colleague and a friend? Ask yourself the question: does the relationship sustain itself, regardless of the environment? Often, if you change church or change your job, most of your relationships from these environments will slowly die away – they were just acquaintances and colleagues. But if any of the relationships continue, they were probably genuine friendships. The relationship itself was the reason for the friendship, not the activity or the environment it happened in.

Friendship is not necessarily about being an extrovert, or having people in and out of your house all the time. Nigel and Paula knew lots of people. Their house was always full. Yet in chatting to them one day, it became clear that actually they were very lonely. They had no real friends, just a myriad of people who came and went. On one level, this was good for them. But the deeper listening, the deeper sharing, those unspoken deeper commitments, never took place – and they felt the pain of this.

If you're going to make friends, it will take a little focus and effort. But there is no doubt that you and they will be healthier and more whole people because of those friendships.

Even though the examples I have given here are of married people, the fact is that whether or not you are single or married, you need friends. You need to put the effort into friendship making. We all need to apply these friend-ship principles to our lives.

A lot of psychologists have written in great depth about this subject. Mother Teresa, when visiting Great Britain many years ago, commented that she had never seen so many lonely people as she had seen then on the streets of London.

Dealing with dysfunction

All of us, whether single or married, are in danger of collecting dysfunctional habits, which at some point are going to come out in our relationships with other people and cause us problems. It would be a good discipline for all of us, whether married or single, to keep an eye on the underlying dysfunctions that might be in our lives. As a single person, we may have the privilege, because we are not living necessarily in an environment with other people, that our underlying character dysfunctions may not be so evident. But obviously marriage and family give an environ-ment for these problems to come out. Therefore, most of the stories that I am using to illustrate this will relate to marriages, but some of the following stories and examples are very important for singles to think about as well. The challenge of intimacy is important for us all, and the skills that build it.

So before hard times happen to any of us – and this applies particularly to married couples, but not exclusively so – let us think about the possible dysfunctions we have in our characters and lives and seek to keep the dysfunctions to a minimum. Most marriages have at least one if not a number of dysfunctions. These can develop over a number of years, and sometimes it is easier to live with the problems than deal with them – to sweep them under the carpet.

In a sense, you are consenting adults, so if the dysfunctions aren't a major problem, why not live with them? The answer is that it's perfectly fine to live with them when you can handle them. But if a real problem comes along, you now have a compounded problem. The problem, plus your dysfunctions, sometimes means that there is not enough energy or trust for you to work together as a couple to overcome the problem properly. The underlying dysfunction has to be dealt with first, before you can even start on the problem.

Ailish and I had to deal with the underlying dysfunction of my non-confrontational nature, and my undermining of her authority, before we could even start with the problems we were facing with our son. We were fortunate in that we had built up some good friendships, had strong and close connections to church, cell and pastors, and had a daily habit of praying together. When disaster struck, the dysfunction did strain the relationship, but our strengths sustained us as we worked through the problem.

What is dysfunctional in your relationship? And are you honest enough to deal with it? Sometimes these dysfunctions are in areas called blind spots. They are glaringly obvious to everyone but you. And sometimes they are not dealt with, because when husbands, wives or others have sought to point them out, they appear so unreal or unimportant to you that they are dismissed out of hand. What does it matter if you are a little opinionated? Does it make a huge difference if you can't really confront people?

The answer is yes and no. The odd instance here and there will make no difference at all. But a habit of a lifetime might build unnecessary strain and stress into a relationship, and will make things very difficult when real trouble comes.

Let us look at some common areas of dysfunction in marriage. Intimacy is one. Most women will tell you that what they long for most in relationships is intimacy. But according to research that has been done both in America and in the United Kingdom, the average man spends less than 14 minutes a week in eye-to-eye contact with his partner, asking questions and really listening to what is happening in her life. Listening and speaking skills, which are fundamental to good relationships, are fast becoming a dying art.

One couple I knew were having some real problems: anger, throwing things around, and very little evidence of a positive relationship with each other. When they sought help, many of their problems were traced back to the fact that although the young man in question did love his wife he knew nothing about intimacy. He spent no time listening, asking questions and finding out about her wants and desires. They had been caught up in the treadmill of life.

When marriage counsellors talk to couples where the woman has a low sex drive, or emotions and feelings have totally disappeared, in the end it often comes back to the fact that the man is not naturally relational, and being intimate is hard work for him. In general, men find their sense of significance in what they do. Women, however, find significance in their relationships. This is why there is a need for intimacy.

A useful tool to help build intimacy is the art of asking good questions. If you ask someone, 'Did you have a good day?' and they answer with either 'yes' or 'no', what have you learned? Nothing! But if you ask questions like: 'What did you do today?' and 'What was the high point?' or 'What was the low point?' you will get a response that is more personal.

Remember, though: when listening to the answer, do not watch the telly, avoid the temptation of reading the newspaper that is five feet away on the floor, and don't disappear into your own imagination, leaving a rather vague expression on your face.

Sometimes you might personally find the answers to your questions boring. That is not the point. The point is that this is what this person's life has been about on this particular day. By asking questions and listening, you give worth to that person, and this builds intimacy.

A dysfunction in your relationship might be sex-related. Too much, too little, too this, too that. Sometimes the lack of intimacy for some women means that their sexual drive is not as strong as it might otherwise be. A vicious circle begins to take place. The man is disgruntled because there's not enough sexual activity. The wife is disgruntled because there's not enough intimacy. Around and around the mulberry bush everybody goes. In the end, this is one of those dysfunctions that people just sometimes leave alone. It is too difficult to deal with.

Another dysfunction that runs through many relationships is attitudes towards money: the spender versus the hoarder. This can cause a lot of friction and arguments.

But perhaps no area is more important in a marriage than children. If you have them, they can – as you have seen from my story – be a great cause of pain. You can avoid some of that by appropriate investment in them as they grow up – investment of time, care and love. But please don't fall into a guilt trap if your children cause problems or go off the rails. You may have been perfectly faithful in investing time in them, and their going off the rails might not be your fault.

Let us look at some guidelines that will help you in your relationship with your children, and hopefully avoid pain in the future.

The first thing to do is recognise your inadequacy. Most of us are far more ignorant about how children operate, and the best way to parent them, than we think we are. While most of us will buy a book that takes us through the stages of pregnancy and childbirth, very few of us will buy books that deal with the next stages: how to parent toddlers, juniors or teenagers.

If we need skills and experience in our jobs and other important areas of our lives, it is a little naïve to think that we don't need the same amount of training and equipping for being a parent. That which has been modelled to us by our own parents may not be adequate for today's children.

The simple answer to this is: learn. Read the right books at the right time. When you see parents who seem to have done a good job, ask them questions: 'Why do you think your children turned out the way they did? What did you do that helped that process?' Similarly, when you meet people you admire, ask them what their parents did right to help them become who they are.

I could probably write a whole book about this, but here are just two simple principles that might be helpful.

One, children need parents, and parents should be in control, in the right sense of the word. Boundary setting is an important part of the development of children, though how you set those boundaries and the consequences you impose to reinforce them will vary from family to family.

The most important guideline about boundary setting – which I have learned from hard experience – is that the parents need to be in agreement. Children have an instinctive feel for when one parent has different standards or boundaries from the other. They will play parent off against parent with a consummate skill that in a four-year-old is nothing short of amazing. By their teenage years, they will have honed this down to a fine art!

At a very early age in the children's lives, the parents need to realise that it is not so much what the boundaries are but that they have to be in agreement about them, and also about the consequences that will follow if they are broken. This is as true for a four-year-old as it is for a teenager.

With a younger child, you will set the boundary without negotiation or discussion. With a fourteen- or fifteen-year-old, you may want to involve them in the process of boundary setting. For example, your sixteen-year-old will say to you, 'Everybody drinks some alcohol at the party. Can't I?'

You might agree and say, 'Yes, you can drink one beer or two. But if you come home drunk, you will be grounded for a month' – or whatever consequence you see fit. Then you must stick to what you said. Having set that boundary, if it is violated the consequence must follow.

Boundary setting produces security in children. It is a tangible way for them to know they are loved. You might think you show love to your children by not setting boundaries and being abstract in the way you parent – again I am talking from experience – but the fact is that the worst thing for a child is to be without accountability, much as they tell you they want to be and push at the boundaries.

The second principle to remember about children is that they need relationships and intimacy just as much as adults. Of course, the nature of this intimacy will change as the child grows and develops. What is appropriate for a four-year-old is not necessarily appropriate for a fourteen-year-old. Nevertheless, in different ways they need the intimacy and relationship of parents or parent, as the case may be.

The language of intimacy has three important ingredients in it: touch and physical affection; listening, with eye-to-eye contact; and time and activities together. These three ingredients are vital in showing your love and developing relationships with your children. With a baby, there will be a great deal of touching and holding, along with talking and activity together. With a teenager, there may be very little touching, but a lot more asking questions and listening.

It might be worth noting that with teenagers, quantity of time is more important than quality. Teenagers seem to go through a stage when they want their parents – particularly boys with fathers – just to hang out with them. In these 'hang out' times, there might be very little meaningful conversation. Just the fact that you are together, and that the parent is prepared to be bored and make sacrifices for the child, communicates great value.

A father called Tim was going through a difficult time with his son. The relationship had become very distant, and there was obviously a problem under the surface. The one thing his son was keen on was the occasional visit up the motorway to an arcade, followed by a bacon sandwich, normally at about eleven at night when this boy should really have been in bed. As this was the only time Tim was able to get with his son, he made a commitment to respond positively to this lifeline.

It always seemed to happen when Tim was feeling extraordinarily tired and the last thing he wanted to do was spend two hours in a daft motorway arcade, followed by a bacon sandwich he didn't need to eat. In these two hours, hardly a word would be said. Nevertheless, after Tim had done this for a period of time, when they were coming back from one arcade session particularly late at night, Tim's son, for the very first time, started a conversation that had meaning and depth. The conversation gave some clues as to why the difficulties had arisen.

In retrospect, the visits to the arcade were worth their weight in gold. They were the pathway to the resolution, and the positive relationship that Tim now has with his son.

On a related note, all human relationships are made in the context of something else. If you want to make friends out there in the world, join a squash club or participate in a common activity. This way, acquaintances over a period of time develop into friendships, and you have created relationship bridges.

In evangelism, though, remember that if you have a new relationship, which is the equivalent of a one-tonne relationship bridge, don't drive a five-tonne gospel truck all over it, as the relationship will crumble. Don't go shooting off hardhitting Bible verses and fiery gospel challenges when the relationship isn't ready for it.

This same simple principle is true of all relationships. Even with your children, you need to create a positive context to build relationships. And you need to be sensitive to the strength of the relationship bridge, and not drive a five-tonne correction or consequence over a one-tonne bridge.

This is particularly true for step-parents. If you are a stepfather or stepmother, you have to create a context, other than just being the step-parent, to build a relationship. One of the foundations of all relationships is trust. Trust is one of those funny things that has to be built up slowly, and often it happens in the fun things and the relational things of life. You say you will do something and you do it. You listen to the other person and show them value. You are placing, by small acts of kindnesses, by eye contact, by doing what you say you will do, a foundation into the relationship. If you seek to put a weight on that foundation by saying to the other person, 'You can't do this, or you can't go there,' or some other demand, then you will crack the foundations and your hard work is undone. In the building of new relationships, make sure that the demand is appropriate to the depth of trust and understanding.

I experienced for myself what it feels like to have a stepfather, even though I was a young adult at the time. Bill was his name, and he was wise enough to know that he needed to spend a considerable period of time developing a relationship with me before he had any right to push traffic over the bridge that he was building.

After a number of years, trust was established, and every now and then he pushed a little something over that relationship bridge. Sadly, he has now died. After twenty years of his being my stepfather, I miss his counsel and wisdom.

It is important to note that in our postmodern world, positional authority is not what it once was. Whether you are a church leader, a step-parent or a natural parent, you will have far more authority in someone's life through relationships, and the rights you've earned in those relationships, than through your position.

Positional authority is based on the concept that you have truth that no one else does. In today's world, where truth is not seen as it once was, experience and relationship are much more highly valued. Truth *is* important, but you will have to convey that truth through means of relationships, rather than by position.

So let's go and build relationships with our children – and with people out there in the world.

10

Living in Hope

If you want an extraordinary story of a group of people who had great hope in the midst of pain and suffering, just look at the first 300 years of the Church. There have been many times of persecution and difficulty for the Christian Church in the last two millennia, but for those very early Christians it was even more difficult. They did not have a history to look back to, or a worldwide fellowship to help them. This new Church of Jesus Christ was under persecution the length and breadth of the Roman Empire.

Recently, historians have re-emphasised the dynamic hope of the early Church. Findings show that the primary message they preached was one of hope for tomorrow as a result of their faith in Christ. Symbols they used included the anchor and the dove, as well as many pictures of Jesus the Shepherd. These symbols can be seen in the catacombs of Rome, and they give us a very accurate picture of how the early Christians lived in hope.

It is interesting to note that the cross, which is the most important symbol of the Church today, did not become a significant symbol of the Church until the third century. The symbols of the early Church had more to do with resurrection, with heaven and with hope.

In some of the writings of the early church fathers, and also from other historical documents, you can see that these early Christians lived as citizens of heaven – which was their hope – and not as citizens of earth. They fully entered into life about them, but they lived that life in the light of their hope.

To give you a picture of this, here is a description of the early Christians from the 'Letter to Diognetus' (an apology by an unknown author of the second century):

> They live in their own countries and are strangers. They loyally fulfil their duties as citizens, but are treated as foreigners. Every foreign land is for them a fatherland and every fatherland, foreign.
>
> They marry like everyone, they have children, but they do not abandon their new-born. They have the table in common, but not the bed. They are in the flesh, but do not live according to the flesh. They dwell on earth, but are citizens of heaven.

The early Christians believed that the quality of their lives proved the beauty of their religion and faith. We can see this in a quote from the 'Books to Autolicus' of St Theophilus of Antioch in the second century:

> We find out that Christians have a wise self-control, practise temperance, marry only once, keep chaste, refuse injustice, uproot sin, practice justice, observe the law, have a positive appreciation of piety. God is acknowledged, and truth is regarded as the supreme law.

Here is another picture of the early Church, from the 'Apology' by Aristides, also written in the second century:

> Christians bear the divine laws impressed on their hearts and observe them in the hope of a future life. For this reason they do not commit adultery, or fornication; don't bear false witness; don't misappropriate the money they have received on deposit; don't crave for what is not due to them; honour father and mother; do good to their neighbour; and when they are appointed judges, judge rightly.
>
> They help those who offend them, making friends of them; do good to their enemies. They don't adore idols; they are kind, good, modest, sincere, they love one another; don't despise widows; protect the orphans; those who have much give without grumbling to those in need. When they meet strangers, they invite them to their homes with joy, for they recognise them as true brothers, not natural but spiritual.
>
> When a poor man dies, if they become aware, they contribute according to their means for his funeral; if they come to know that some people are persecuted or sent to prison or condemned for the sake of Christ's name, they put their alms together and send them to those in need. If they can do it, they try to obtain their release. When a slave or a beggar is in need of help, they fast two or three days and give him the food they had prepared for themselves, because they think that he too should be joyful, as he has been called to be joyful like themselves.
>
> They strictly observe the commandments of the Lord,

by living in a saintly and right way, as the Lord God has prescribed to them; they give Him thanks each morning and evening for all food and drink and every other thing.

As you read these incredible accounts, it is not surprising that the early Church changed the face of the earth. Christianity spread like wildfire. You don't see people living under the cloud of pain and disillusionment and death. In fact, you see the exact opposite: people who experienced pain and difficulty every day, but lived in the light of their hope and confidence.

In this book we have looked at the storms, but to the early Church the anchor was a symbol of hope. Think of a ship being tossed to and fro, yet it will not be driven on to the shores if the anchor is set true. For us, we set our anchor true by having the right value systems.

There is a difference between Christian hope and human enthusiasm. Christian hope is not a false confidence, here today and gone tomorrow. It is an abiding sense of the presence of God that transcends the difficulties of today and looks to tomorrow. Human enthusiasm, or false confidence, is limited by our human capacity and is easily deflated.

Many years ago, I had a dog called Hovis – the well-bread dog! He had, I am sad to say, an extremely mean disposition. In today's climate, he would have been put down, as his attitude was to bite first and ask questions later. The list of his victims was long.

On one particular day, some building work was being done on our house. A lorry driver arrived, and the builders warned him that there was a very dangerous dog on the site. His mind immediately conjured up images of savage Rottweilers and dangerous Alsatians.

Eventually, he asked, 'What kind of dog is it?'

'A sausage dog,' they replied.

The lorry driver couldn't stop laughing. 'You're afraid of a sausage dog? One swing of my boot and it will be history.'

He got out of the lorry and walked into the house. Hovis was sitting in his normal place at the end of the corridor. This was because he liked a long run-up before he assailed his victims. As the driver came in, Hovis set off, barking furiously.

The man was as good as his word – he swung his foot with all his might. If he had connected, this story would have had a different conclusion. But Hovis had seen this sort of thing many times before. He leaned slightly sideways as the boot passed his ear, then bit the man hard in the Achilles tendon, separated it in three places, and the man spent three weeks in hospital having microsurgery to restore it.

The driver had false confidence. So can we – here today and gone tomorrow. But Christians are to develop an anchor for their soul – a hope that sustains them, no matter how dark the storm or rough the water.

> May the God of hope fill you with all joy and peace in believing, so that you may abound in hope by the power of the Holy Spirit.
>
> (Romans 15:13)

One element of this scripture is that the God of all hope will fill you with joy and peace.

Despite all the selfishness and pain in the world, God has opened up a pathway of hope for you through Christ. Hope is about relationship with God in the now, that you can know God and experience his peace and forgiveness.

But hope is also a promise for the future. In heaven there will be no more tears and no more sadness. So what do you have to do to secure this hope?

The answer is to be found in another element in this scripture: you must believe. This is the difficult part. At the heart of Christianity is a challenge – to believe what you cannot see; to trust in the love of God when you don't feel it's there; and to believe that God is with you, even when evidence and circumstances indicate otherwise.

In Hebrews we read that 'faith is the assurance of things hoped for, the conviction of things not seen' (Hebrews 11:1). Our belief in hope is the foundation of the Christian faith. Our faith says that things that are *not* seen are more real than that which *is* seen.

Throughout history, Christians have hoped for things that they may never have actually seen. Abraham hoped for a promised land, which he never fully entered into. Saints have suffered horrible deaths, yet hope was in their hearts.

For some, their hope was fulfilled in this world. In the case of Moses, the Red Sea was parted and the Egyptian persecutors were drowned. Likewise, the early Church pursued its course of hope, and within three centuries, the Roman Empire was changed by the power of the gospel message.

You need hope in different ways. You need to have hope that the presence of God is with you. You need to have hope about what your life can achieve. You need hope for the future of the Church. You need hope for the nation.

The amazing thing is that your believing gives you power. The final element of this scripture in Romans says that the power of the Holy Spirit will abound in the hope that you have. Hope is the foundation of faith.

In preparing for tomorrow's pain and disillusionment, think about your own personal walk with God and ask yourself, 'Where am I in my walk? Am I moving forward?' There is a helpful framework in 1 John that might guide you in this process.

> I am writing to you, little children, because your sins are forgiven for his sake. I am writing to you, fathers (and mothers), because you know him who is from the beginning. I am writing to you, young men (and women), because you have overcome the evil one. I write to you, children, because you know the Father. I write to you, fathers (and mothers), because you know him who is from the beginning. I write to you, young men (and women), because you are strong, and the word of God abides in you, and you have overcome the evil one.
>
> (1 John 2:12–14; the words in brackets are mine)

In this, you see three stages of spiritual development: little children; young men and women; and spiritual mothers and fathers. It is important that you work your way through these stages in a sequential manner, even though at times there will be a little bit of overlap.

Little children

The first stage of spiritual development is when you are like 'little children'. There are two important characteristics to this stage. One is that you begin to experience your sins being forgiven. The second is that you know the Father; you know God.

Unfortunately, the forgiveness aspect of this can often be short-circuited. Many people have come to faith using a conversion prayer with a very generalised approach to forgiveness: 'Lord, forgive me all my sins. Amen.'

God does hear these prayers, and there *is* a level of interaction and forgiveness. But this approach means that people miss out on two important things that should be happening.

The first is the principle found in 1 John:

> If we confess our sins, he who is faithful and just will forgive us our sins and cleanse us from all unrighteousness.
>
> (1 John 1:9)

The word 'confess' here is the Greek work *homeo logio*. This means literally that we need to say the same thing – in other words, speak out our specific sins. This is a more painful process than the blanket conversion prayer. We have to call our sins what they are: 'Lord, please forgive me for my anger.'

Many years ago, I was involved in leading a young man to the Lord. I asked him to confess just one thing he knew God was unhappy with in his life. This he did. He confessed that he had beaten up an old lady. The pain of his confession showed him how horrible his actions had been, and there was a genuine desire in him to be different. His values were changing.

This is what happens when you confess things specifically. You realise exactly what you have done, and the realisation gives you momentum to turn away from them.

The second important thing about forgiveness is found in the words of Jesus:

> Therefore, I tell you, her sins, which were many, have been forgiven; hence she has shown great love. But the one to whom little is forgiven, loves little.
>
> (Luke 7:47)

Jesus is saying that those who have been forgiven much end up loving much. Sometimes you can be robbed of loving much, of really knowing the love of God, because you have taken the blanket approach to forgiveness.

I can remember a painful day many years ago, when I spent the whole day confessing many of the bad thoughts that had been in my mind due to reading pornography as a youth. When I sensed God's forgiveness at the end of that day, I was amazed at how much God loved me. That experience of being forgiven was a bedrock for my future life.

As I mentioned before, an important characteristic of the 'little children' stage of spiritual development is that you know the Father. You don't have to work at knowing God. You don't have to do great deeds. This is not an earned relationship. An unparalleled, amazing gift from God is that we know him.

So, young Christians have this wonderful experience of being forgiven and knowing God. You could call this stage of your Christian walk the receiving stage. Obviously, there will be times, even in maturity, when you will be receiving and experiencing God in this way. But in general terms, you cannot remain at this stage.

It is a wonderful thing to see young children receiving and being spoilt by the love of their parents, but teenagers with the same attitude are not attractive. It is the same when you are a Christian. You must move on.

In our current culture, with its emphasis on consumerism, sometimes the way we do church encourages people to stay in the receiving mode. But the challenge is to move on to the next stage in your spiritual journey.

Young men and women

This next stage is where you will spend a great deal of your life. As with 'little children', there are a number of characteristics that describe this stage. One of them is that young men and young women have overcome the evil one.

> I write to you, young men (and women), because you are strong, and the word of God abides in you, and you have overcome the evil one.
>   (1 John 2:14; the words in brackets are mine)

Overcoming the evil one means overcoming those life-controlling habits that have been holding you back, whether they are anger, self-centredness, laziness, lust, or whatever. This is not to say that you will be entering into a period of marvellous perfection. There will still be days when you will make mistakes. But in essence, you are aiming for a new level of maturity.

Overcoming the evil one also means that you are reaching out – by living out your Christian faith in your day-to-day life from Monday to Friday, and also in church. You are seeking to exercise the destiny God has for you. Your desire is to be obedient to the opportunities and possibilities you have to live a Christ-like life: to love God, love one another and love the lost. You are not a passive Christian but a mobile and active one.

The essence of being a young man or woman is that you meet God in your activity. Being a spiritual child is about receiving, but being a young man or woman is about doing. As you seek to overcome your personal weaknesses, you meet with God. As you seek to put the personal values of the scriptures into your life, you meet with God. As you go out to do the things he has called you to do, you also meet with God. He is there.

Another characteristic of this stage involves being strong, with the word of God abiding in you. It's not just about reading the scriptures. You need to take the principles behind the scriptures and make them the bedrock and foundations of your life.

An important indication that the word of God abides in you and you have reached a level of Christian maturity is that you believe that God is who he says he is, and that he is with you, regardless of your circumstances and what your feelings or emotions are telling you. Until you come to this conviction, your Christian life will have a yo-yo dimension to it, with lots of ups and downs. You will be shaped by your external circumstances, rather than your internal convictions.

Spiritual parents

The third stage of your spiritual development is that you become a spiritual mother or father. This is the great need of the Church today.

The only thing the scripture in 1 John says about spiritual mothers and fathers is that they know God. This is said twice. In essence, this stage is not about receiving or doing, but being. It is about knowing God for who he is in his own right, with no obligation for God to meet you in terms of receiving or doing. You are developing your relationship with God, not for what you can get out of it, not so that you can have some wonderful experiences, but purely for its own sake – to know him and understand the ways of God more.

In Psalm 103:7 we read: 'He made known his ways to Moses, his acts to the people of Israel.'

In the first two stages of your Christian life, you experience the acts of God. That's not bad. In fact, it's wonderful. But Moses was a spiritual father. He was a friend of God, and he understood God's ways and why he did things. The challenge for you is, like Moses, to move on in friendship with God.

In some ways, you might think that this would be the easiest part of your Christian life. But actually it is the hardest, mainly because of what I've spent much of this book talking about. On your journey from being a spiritual child to becoming a spiritual parent, you've been around long enough to see through the froth and the bubble. You have lots of questions, and you know that there won't be many easy answers. You've seen things in church that never should have happened, and you've ended up with a certain amount of spiritual baggage, including pain and disillusionment.

Spiritual mothers or fathers do not deny the reality of this pain and disillusionment. Instead, they meet with God in the midst of it. Through many times of heartache and pain, they have pushed forward to know God more.

This is not to judge those who, for whatever reason, have got stuck on the journey. Sometimes it seems that there are just as many downs as ups. This is perfectly normal. There will be ups and downs on your Christian journey, but in the long run you are getting higher.

The encouragement to be found in Psalm 103 is that God can be known. He is telling us: 'Come on, that's it, higher.' Yes, it's been difficult, but here is the most wonderful goal to aim for: to know God, and to know him more.

Our nation is turning dark. Society's values are changing rapidly, and a Christian way of life is being abandoned. Commitment, honesty, integrity, family – many of the virtues and wonders of our faith have shaped and made our society a better place, but these are being lost.

Never before has there been such a need for spiritual mothers and fathers – people who, because they have been there and because they know God, can pray for and encourage this generation with realism and integrity. They can form the spiritual backbone that will see a reformation in this land, a change within society.

In the end, this is your challenge. Will you be one of

those people? Will you be a spiritual parent? Can you move beyond the clouds, to know God more and to make him known in this world?

Appendix 1

Justyn's Story

What and how did I feel?

I definitely look back on my teenage years with mixed emotions. To try and summarise how I felt during these years is very difficult for me. What I will do is look at three different areas to do with my emotional state at the time.

First, there was the resentment I had towards my father. This was made worse by a trusted Christian youth worker's negative influence on me. He showed me love and affection through just 'hanging out' with me. This was something I felt my father never did. However, my time with this youth worker was definitely a stimulus to continue my rebellion, especially as he never discouraged my bad attitude towards my father.

Second, I felt isolated and needed attention. I remember one time at the age of ten, when my father was very busy, he told me to 'fight my own battles'. He did not realise the significance of this. I never forgot what he said, and soon had a philosophy of complete dependence on myself. Nothing could affect me, and no one could get near me.

On the inside, though, I was insecure and desperate, longing for attention. That is why I thrived on getting attention through disruptive behaviour. Being uncontrollable and controlling the family – and succeeding at it – only made me want to continue. It made me feel important. But on the inside I was hurt and angry, and all this attention-seeking was just a way to cover up my hurt emotions.

Third, I experienced regret. Secretly, I disliked – *hated* – the trouble I was getting into and the pain it was causing my family, especially my mother. On the inside, I never wanted to do the things I did. I hated the way I was, with all my insecurities, and the pain and suffering I was causing.

What helped me change?

Again, there are many different factors to look at in answering this question. One was my willingness to change in the first place. Much of what helped me get to this place was the encouragement I received from others, and the realisation that I could succeed as a person. Dad often showed how proud he was of me when I did well, even in the midst of my disruptive behaviour. My mother always made it clear that she hated my ways, but could never hate *me* and loved me dearly.

A change in friendship groups was fundamental. The friends I had before were never real friends. I was just the class clown who made them laugh. As my security grew stronger through a realisation that I could do well in school, my confidence grew, along with my academic skills, and my friendship groups changed.

I became more aware of social skills, and began to take more time and care in what I said to people. For this to happen, a strong set of friends is needed. Security isn't built around the number of friends you've got, but the quality of friendship.

For me, it wasn't just school friends, but people in leadership who could be fully trusted. After the disastrous experience with the first youth worker, I found it very difficult to trust authority figures. Yet at the age of fifteen, I was blessed by two very strong and anointed youth workers (Tré and Trent Sheppard) who had a lot of time for me and genuinely cared.

So, change came from a willingness in myself to change, a realisation of self-worth, and strong and stable friendship groups.

One thing I didn't do at this time was give much credit to Father God. From the age of thirteen to sixteen, when I did most of my changing, I had little to do with Christianity. It wasn't until much later on, through a moment of 'coincidence' – which I believe was arranged by God – that I was able to speak briefly with a lady called Joy Dawson. She highlighted where God had had his hand on my life in previous years, even though I hadn't acknowledged him. People had been praying for me all through my life, even when I didn't know they were.

I now have no doubt that my change of friends, my youth leaders, my Attention Deficit Hyperactivity Disorder (ADHD) diagnosis and the medicine, were all part of God's plan. Due to that, all the glory must go to him.

The medication I took for the ADHD played a big part in the progress I made at school. My academic work improved dramatically, largely due to the medicine helping me to concentrate. But I still had to make a conscious decision to turn up to class, do my work and hand it in on time. Medication or no medication, a choice had to be made. The medication helped, but I still had to make the decision to reach my full potential at school, which I would encourage everybody to do.

Improvement in my father's relationship with me

One of the problems that I found with my dad was the way in which he seldom drew boundaries and was inefficient with sticking to rules and punishment which he had set. This meant that I was able to get my own way much of the time. Throughout my early teenage years I got into much drinking and partying and such things, things far from the life God intended.

In recently reading Galatians 5 in *The Message* version of the Bible, I was astounded at how much this passage related to my life throughout my teenage years and how it particularly related to the authority figures in my life.

> It is obvious what kind of life develops out of trying to get your own way all the time: repetitive, loveless, cheap sex; a stinking accumulation of mental and emotional garbage; frenzied and joyless grabs for happiness; trinket gods, magic-show religion; paranoid loneliness; cutthroat competition; all-consuming-yet-never-satisfied wants; a brutal temper; an impotence to love or be loved; divided homes and divided lives; small-minded and lopsided pursuits; the vicious habit of depersonalising everyone into a rival; uncontrolled and uncontrollable addictions; ugly parodies of community.
>
> Galatians 5:19–21 (*The Message*)

These are just a few of the acts which an uncontrollable home life could and often does lead to. Many of them were true in my life. However, the most destructive one for me was depersonalising everyone into a rival. This was very true with my dad. Dad wanted to be my best mate, yet I saw him as number one enemy. As soon as you lose respect for your own father, as I did, you become almost fearless. Once you know you can get away with aggressive, truculent behaviour at home, you will take those attitudes with you wherever you go. That loss of authority in the home leads to a multitude of difficulties outside the home.

The Bible talks about freedom from all these bondages through living out the fruit of the Spirit and inviting Christ to live in us. The facets of patience, faithfulness and love were the greatest catalysts for growth in Dad's relationship with me improving.

Another factor was my dad's faithfulness. He was faithful to trust God, that God could and would bring a transformation as long as I recognised the need for God to bring a change in me. God started to work considerably in my life, even though change is a lengthy process.

Another factor in my difficulties was a lack of self-control – one of the facets of the fruit of the Spirit which *The Message* version translates as 'the ability to marshal energies wisely'. So many times in school reports I would receive comments like, 'Justyn has much energy and enthusiasm, if only he could channel it in the right direction.'

There isn't one thing that we can say is the right way to marshal these energies, but what I found is that there had to be a switch in what I spent my time doing. The focus of my activities needed to be in line with what Jesus would do, and when I didn't do that the sins referred to earlier from Galatians 5 would occur. If we focus our lives on Jesus he will use our talents, skills and energies in the most constructive and beneficial ways for us and for his glory.

It's taken a long time for me to make Jesus the focus of my life, but in the meantime Dad took the initiative in getting involved with what I was interested in. The point was that he showed a genuine interest and was willing to spend time to work on rebuilding our relationship. Any common interest which unites is valuable as it acts as a stepping stone for that friendship to be built on. A crucial part for me and my father was him cutting back on travel to spend time with me and the family. This was a key catalyst on the road to the recovery of our relationship.

Some advice to parents

If you are a parent, remember that if your son or daughter is expressing rebellion through things like smoking, swearing, drinking or getting into fights, it doesn't necessarily mean they are fulfilled by them. These rebellious acts might be covering up real issues for them – don't just look at the acts, look at what's behind them.

You need to acknowledge that your child might feel isolated. His or her insecurity might be bigger than you can possibly imagine. If the child seems tough and self-reliant on the outside, then inwardly – and this is my own experience – that child is desperate and longing for something more. Their sense of security has to be built up, and real encouragement and genuine evidence of love is needed. As Billy Graham said, 'Children spell love T–I–M–E.' The lack of time Dad spent with me as a child contributed to the lack of love and isolation which I felt. Even though Dad did always love me, that love had to be shown in more ways than just words.

Although I think parents have to draw clear boundaries and guidelines on what is and what isn't acceptable, they have to be patient as transformation doesn't come overnight. Also, any boundary setting has to be acted out in love – showing raw anger to an obnoxious teenager is never constructive. That's why love is important, as everything you do with your children has to stem from love. Whether it be punishment or free time with your children, it should all be done out of love, not because it seems the right thing to do or from any sense of obligation.

However outwardly bad your child might be, his or her inner potential is incalculable. If he or she is as desperate as I was, they will definitely have the will to change.

There has been much improvement in my life in the last five years, but there are still many slip-ups, such as occasionally blowing up in class. Be assured that the disruptive behaviour does gradually decline, as the child matures and learns self-control. At the age of nineteen I'm still finding it difficult to control my tongue and some of my actions. Dramatic changes do and will happen, but not overnight. Parents have to be very patient, and recognise and encourage any signs of improvement.

At the end of the day, the glory is God's. But for his glory to be revealed, a choice has to be made in the child to change. God's grace, love and perfect timing do the rest.

Some advice to kids

Help and support through God, family and friends is always going to be available. But you have to make a decision in your own heart to move away from a life of desperation and madness to a life of fulfilment. You have to believe in your own potential.

All kids have the potential to do well. If your 'doing well' isn't up to other people's standards, that's not what matters. You still have the ability to do your best. If you find yourself misbehaving to get some attention, wouldn't it be better to do things that make you feel good inside?

When I started working hard at school and stopped getting into fights, I found myself with very few friends. Yet the position I'm in now is far more fulfilling than where I'd be if I'd continued the way I was, which was selfishly centred around getting attention from others.

It's weird how the two things I mocked and laughed at when I was twelve are now so fundamental in my life. The first is God. The second is the people I used to laugh at. My best friends now are the people I used to bully at the age of twelve. I bullied them because deep down I realised that they knew their potential and were getting far more from life than I was.

Tied in with God and friends are youth leaders. One of my closest friends is a youth leader who I know will always stand with and support me. But for years I never trusted anything connected with the Church. In fact, I despised anything that was church-related. Yet now, the Church and the people in it – and certainly God our Father – are my biggest securities.

To conclude, I encourage you again to do the best you possibly can and fulfil the potential God has for you. For this to happen, you have to make the decision to focus on what is important, and work hard to make a change. You also have to believe in yourself, that you can do well in school and do well socially, however hard this may seem. Believe me, if you don't make a choice to change, I doubt much improvement will occur.

Thank you

A big shout goes out to the Venture crew, Brooker, Smithy, all my YWAM friends, not forgetting Bowers for the hand he played in helping me process my thoughts and also what God was telling me throughout this chapter. Particular thanks to Jimmy, the Sheppard brothers and the Sullie boys, who have always been there and not given up on my true potential. Thanks for all the encouragement.

I can also never forget my little sister, Laura, and my big sister, Kiera, who had to be so patient with me during difficult circumstances, and my mum.

Appendix 2

Questions and Reflections

These questions are designed for cell groups/small groups, and in a sense are trying to raise an answer to the following questions:

1 What is the main principle of the chapter? What do I understand?
2 What is its application to everyday life?
3 Who needs help? How can we help one another to put these things into practice?

Feel free to make up your own questions and think through the applications, but below is a chapter-by-chapter list of suggested questions and applications. They begin with a personal reflection for the reader.

Chapter 1: It's All Right to Feel Pain – A Personal Story

Personal reflection
Hard times happen to everyone. You're not alone. Many people have experienced the same things you are experiencing. Hard times do not mean that you are a failure or have failed God. Difficulties are a part of life.

Questions for small group/cell

- Discuss whether you think hard times and pain are things that everyone goes through, whether they are Christian or non-Christian.
- If pain comes into your life, what is your most common response?
- What can you learn from Laurence's story?

Chapter 2: Jesus – His Pain and Disillusionment

Personal reflection

Do the sufferings of Jesus bear any similarities to some of the pain and difficulties you have experienced? If so, reflect on the fact that Jesus understands what you're feeling. As you experience pain, suffering and rejection, remember the extraordinary fact that the Godhead has experienced them as well, and understands.

Questions for small group/cell

- Do you really think that God understands the pain and difficulties we face?
- Out of all the difficult experiences that Jesus went through, which do you think were the most traumatic and difficult?
- What can you learn from Jesus' life as you look at how he handled pain and suffering?

Application

Share with each other how you think the suffering of Jesus helps with your own experience of suffering and difficulty.

Chapter 3: Pain – Where Does It Come From?

Personal reflection

It is helpful to ask ourselves the questions: what is the primary source of pain in my life? Where does it come from?

Questions for small group/cell

- What do you think are the most common causes of pain that you have observed?
- How does knowing the source help in dealing with pain?

Chapter 4: Disillusionment – Where Does It Come From?

Personal reflection

Disillusionment is not sin, just a very natural response to the difficult experiences of life.

Questions for small group/cell

- What do you think causes disillusionment?
- What disillusions you the most: things that happen in church, or things that you experience as an individual in your everyday life?

Application

Share some common disillusionments that could affect you, making you live your Christian life differently from the way you would like to live.

Chapter 5: Steps to Freedom from Pain

Personal reflection
Honesty brings freedom. What can you do to put some of the steps or principles from this chapter into practice? Which principle would help you most at this point?

Questions for small group/cell
- Discuss the principles that have been outlined in this chapter. If you can, give a testimony to the group of a principle that has worked in your life.
- Which of these principles do you think are the most important? What can you as a group do to help each other put them in place?
- Do you find one of these principles particularly difficult? Would you like prayer from the group?

Chapter 6: Overcoming Disillusionment

Personal reflection
Am I holding on to rights? What rights should I give over to God?

Questions for small group/cell
- In our world today, the emphasis is on having rights, not giving them up. Discuss the idea of giving up some of our rights.
- Are there rights that we should not give up? Discuss this.

Application
Have an open time of prayer with an opportunity for people to give up any rights they feel God is speaking to them about.

Chapter 7: 'Where is God in All This?'

Personal reflection
Where is the place I feel most comfortable in meeting with God? Perhaps I should go there soon?

Questions for small group/cell
- Discuss the various ways we as a group find God.
- Perhaps different people could share where they meet with God.
- How could we help one another meet with God? Suggest some practical ideas.

Application
Pray for anyone who feels God is far away at the moment. Think of someone you could encourage in the week ahead.

Chapter 8: Spiritual Disciplines

Personal reflection
Is there a value that is weak in my life that might reflect the fact that the corresponding values are not very strong?

Questions for small group/cell
- In what way do you think values are the key to living the Christian life?
- How do you see values making it easier for you to make the right choices?

Application
Of the values Laurence listed, share round in the group which value you think is weakest in your life and pray for one another.

QUESTIONS AND REFLECTIONS

Chapter 9: Preparing for Tomorrow's Pain and Disillusionment

Personal reflection

When things are brought into the light, it helps in the change process. What underlying dysfunction do I need to bring out into the light?

Questions for small group/cell

- What do you think are important foundations that need to be in place in your life so that when difficulties come, they do not overwhelm you?
- Discuss the idea of friendship, especially how you make friends.

Application

Share around the group your response to this question: do I have a friend with whom I am really honest and open, who can speak into my life?

Chapter 10: Living in Hope

Personal reflection

What is my hope for the future? Can I dare to dream again?

Questions for small group/cell

- How could hope in my life be a witness to my non-Christian friends? Discuss what hope we as Christians can offer to the world.

Application
What could we do as a group to demonstrate Christian hope in our community?

Appendix 3

Letter from Iain Muir
to Someone in Pain

Iain Muir is a friend of mine, and a respected Christian leader, who with his wife's death has recently gone through the painful ordeal of bereavement. Since he has experienced a great deal of personal pain, I felt his thoughts, as encompassed in this letter, were significant.

Embracing pain

What do you do with pain? It is an unfriendly invader. It is sharp and untouchable. It doesn't go away easily. Some people turn to other comforts – false comforts – to try to ease the pain. Like alcohol, or drugs, or sex, or food – or even work. But none of these really help. The pain is still inside.

There is another side to pain. It can be turned around to be constructive – like the butterfly struggling to break out of its cocoon. Pain can have positive results, if we deal with it in the right way. Life has joys, lots of them, praise God. But life will always have pain.

We could say that Jesus 'embraced' the cross. A strange

statement. Why would he? You don't embrace what hurts you, the means of your death. Or do you? He embraced the cross. It couldn't really hurt him. Not eternally. Instead, it produced salvation.

When you receive grace to embrace the pain in your life, you take away its power to cause destruction. You stop it from robbing you of years of your life – through the anger, or apathy, or distress that it causes. When you embrace the pain, you begin to see how its effect can be turned into gain. Yes, that saying was right: no pain, no gain.

The pain strips away all that is unreal. We don't want unreality in our lives anyway. Pain uncovers our weak areas so that we can work on them. It exposes those things in us called sin. The stuff we need to get rid of, if our dreams are to come true. But pain also reveals our strengths, the virtues in our lives, the good things we can be thankful for and that we can use to go on and find destiny.

Pain can be a friend. If we embrace it.

'But I do not want to do that. I want to run from pain. Say it's not there. Say it never happened. Tell me it's not true!'

You have to embrace it, or it will never cease to hurt.

Take hold of your pain. Not in a morbid way, not in self-pity, not in despair – but in hope, in love, in a positive way that says, 'I can do this. I can handle it, by God's grace.'

Jesus understands all pain because he suffered all the pain there is. Hurt by his closest. Abandoned to his enemies. He even felt the Father's abandonment – for a moment.

Appendix 4

Definition of ADHD

(Attention Deficit Hyperactivity Disorder)

ADHD is a common but complex medical condition of brain dysfunction that is characterised by excessive inattentiveness, impulsiveness and/or hyperactivity. A diagnosis of ADHD is given when these characteristics significantly interfere with everyday life and are present in both school and home/social situations, and for which there is no other reason.

The condition manifests itself in many ways. In fact, hyperactivity is just one possible feature of the disorder and is often the least of a child's problems. For example, some children may be only inattentive; others may be persistently hyperactive; while for some, hyperactivity will lessen with time.

The wide range of possible presentations can be confusing and there are also many complications that may mask or overshadow the underlying core symptoms and worsen with time. Research shows that ADHD is a genetic, inherited condition that can be effectively managed. The abnormality primarily involves the frontal lobes of the brain and symptoms can be improved by appropriate medication to normal brain function, thereby allowing schooling and other strategies to be more effective. Left untreated, the disorder can interfere significantly with educational and social development and predispose to psychiatric and other difficulties.

ADHD is very variable and can be inconsistent in its presentation. In fact, if a child has ADHD, he or she is more likely to have other co-existing or complication conditions, such as excessive oppositionality and conduct disorder, anxiety and depression, learning difficulties, obsessions, and co-ordination, speech and language difficulties.

There has been a tendency for ADHD to be under-diagnosed and under-appreciated in Britain compared with North America and Australia. Treatment is aimed at allowing the sufferer to lead his or her life more appropriately to potential.

Geoffrey D. Kewley
MB, BS, FRCP, FRCPCH, FRACP, DCH
Consultant Paediatrician/Director
Learning Assessment and Neurocare Centre
Horsham, West Sussex

Notes

1 It was later discovered that this youth worker had major problems and some two years later he was convicted of sexual offences and sent to prison. To our knowledge he is no longer in any form of Christian ministry among young people. His abuse of Justyn was solely of an emotional nature.

2 ADHD has only been diagnosed in fairly recent times and its effect in children is hyperactive behaviour, very limited ability to concentrate (two or three minutes in an hour) and often uncontrollable and dysfunctional behaviour because they tend to react before the control functions and value systems that are in the brain have sent a message to control the behaviour. Children are affected by ADHD to differing degrees. More information in Appendix 4.

3 Edwin Markham, 'The Greater Thing', published in *New Poems: Eighty Songs at 80* (Edwin Markham's fifth book of verse) by Doubleday, Doran & Co., Garden City, New York in 1932.

4 John V. Taylor, *Weep Not For Me: Meditations on the Cross and the Resurrection* (pp. 11–12), copyright © 1986 by the World Council of Churches, WCC Publications, Geneva, Switzerland. Used with permission.

Resources

Books

Attention Deficit Hyperactivity Disorder: Recognition, Reality and Resolution, Dr G. Kewley, David Fulton Publications, 2001.
Understanding Attention Deficit Hyperactivity Disorder, Dr Christopher Green, Vermilion, 1997.

Websites

www.adders.org
Promotes awareness of ADHD.

www.attentiondeficitdisorder.ws/
An ADHD-related links resource.

www.add411.com
An ADHD bookstore.

Centre for Diagnosis

Learning Assessment Centre
2nd Floor
48/50 Springfield Road
Horsham
West Sussex RH12 2PD

Tel: (+44) 01403 240002
e-mail: info@l-a-c.com
Website: www.l-a-c.com

Counselling and reparenting

In addition to referrals by your GP, the *UK Christian Handbook* lists Christian counsellors, marriage courses and reparenting seminars. See www.ukchristianhandbook.org.uk